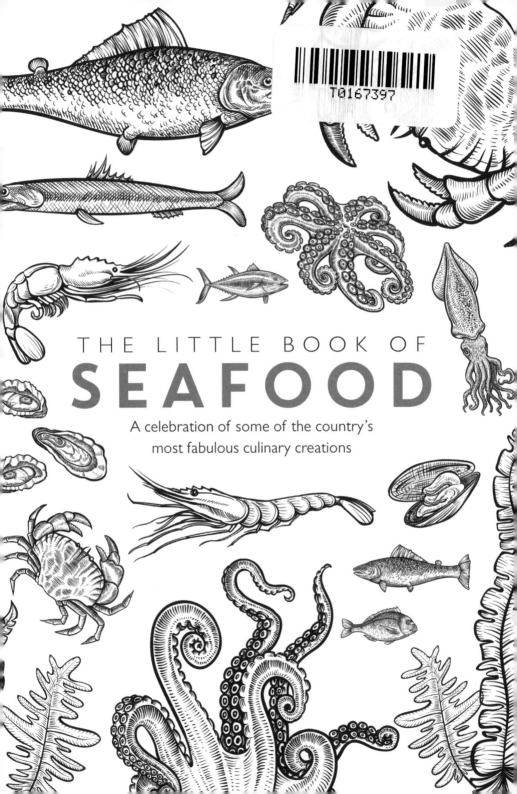

THE LITTLE BOOK OF
SEAFOOD

A celebration of some of the country's
most fabulous culinary creations

©2022 Meze Publishing Ltd.
All rights reserved.

First edition printed in 2022
in the UK.

ISBN: 9781910863978

Edited by: Joe Food, Ash Birch
& Katie Fisher

Designed by: Phil Turner

Compiled by: Emma Toogood

Photography by: Sam Bowles,
Paul Carroll, Aaron Parsons,
Kerry Schofield, Xavier
Buendia, Tim Green, Clair
Irwin, Paul Gregory, Simon
Burt, Marc Barker, Matt
Crowder, Simon Weller.

Contributors: Lizzie Morton,
Megan Hirst, Lizzy Capps

Printed in Great Britain
by Bell and Bain Ltd, Glasgow

me:ze
PUBLISHING

Published by Meze
Publishing Limited

Unit 1b, 2 Kelham Square

Kelham Riverside

Sheffield S3 8SD

Web:
www.mezepublishing.co.uk

Telephone: 0114 275 7709

Email:
info@mezepublishing.co.uk

Contents

Welcome to The Little Book of Seafood

We have scoured the UK for the best artisan producers, fishermen, Michelin-starred restaurants, fish and chip shops, fishmongers, bistros, gastro pubs and many more unique ventures in our 'Get Stuck In' series of regional cook books. The recipes they have produced make up a glorious collection that's too good not to share!

So we have brought the most mouth-watering fish and seafood recipes together from all across the country, celebrating the talent and knowledge of people who do this for a living with pride and passion.

From the north east to the south west, this book showcases regional specialities, classics, contemporary creations and more from independent businesses large and small. In addition to their recipes and stories, you'll find helpful extras including tips and tricks for buying and filleting fish, understanding sustainability and a guide to common types of fish and how to cook them.

Whether you're a novice in the kitchen or a keen experimenter, this book is one to learn from and be inspired by, a go-to compilation for impressing your friends, cooking with your kids and treating your other half (or yourself, of course) to a little bit of indulgence.

Featuring a wide range of seafood specials such as Galton Blackiston's pan fried wild sea bass with squid risotto and nero sauce, showstoppers like Scutchers' fillet of wild turbot with asparagus, broad beans and bacon, and tasty curries including Sri Lankan crab curry from Wells Crabhouse, The Little Book of Seafood has a nautical nibble for every occasion.

The UK's Sustainable Fishing Industry

By The Marine Stewardship Council (MSC)

"Whatever the weather, we go to sea," says Ryan Davey, skipper of the Stelissa hake boat in Newlyn, Cornwall. The sea roils and waves crash onto the bow as the boat makes the arduous 20-hour journey into the Cornish hake fishery, 100 miles off the coast of Newlyn.

Preparing the nets, Ryan says: "to protect the fish stocks, we've adjusted the mesh size of our nets, so that we only catch mature fish." This leaves juvenile fish free to reproduce, an action taken by the fishery to meet the strict requirements of Marine Stewardship Council (MSC) certification, the leading international standard for sustainable fishing.

Thanks to changes brought in by fishers, Cornish hake – a tasty white fish species – has experienced a dramatic comeback since the 1990s, when stocks were left depleted. Receiving MSC certification in 2015 after years of hard work, the fishery is a shining example of how responsible stock management allows for both thriving marine ecosystems and buoyant coastal livelihoods, which have depended on the health and abundance of Cornwall's surrounding waters for decades.

Overfishing sadly remains one of the biggest threats to our oceans, with over a third of global fish stocks overfished. UK waters have been exploited over the years, but the tide is turning. 21 fisheries in the UK and Ireland have been independently certified to the MSC's standard, all of which have made significant efforts to reduce their environmental impact and ensure their respective wild fish populations remain healthy.

Nearly 1000 miles from the Newlyn hake fishery in the pristine waters of the Shetland Islands is the MSC certified Scottish rope-grown mussel fishery. Known for being a low-impact shellfish species, mussels require very little intervention during their growth cycle and thrive when left on the ropes. "It's just nature, we give them a home," says harvester Marvin Thomason.

Scotland's haddock industry is similarly flourishing. The MSC certified haddock fishery is witnessing the biggest numbers of juvenile fish for 40 years. Along with Cornish hake and Shetland mussels, MSC certified Scottish haddock is available to buy in UK supermarkets, distinguishable by the blue MSC ecolabel, which tells consumers that their seafood comes from a sustainable, well-managed fishery.

The MSC is proud to support fishers and their communities who are working tirelessly to ensure longevity for this time-honoured industry, but also to ensure our oceans remain teeming with life for generations to come. There is a fine balance to strike, but as Marvin's brother Christopher puts it, "the sea is on loan, and we'll hand it back as we find it."

Buying and Preparing Shellfish

Buying and Storing

At your fish market, ask the fishmonger for the day's freshest catch. When in doubt, give it the sniff test: clams, oysters and shellfish should smell like the ocean, and that's all. An overly fishy smell means they've been sitting around too long and are past their prime. The shells of fresh clams, oysters, mussels and scallops need to be tightly closed, or just slightly ajar. If they are open a little, they should quickly close when tapped lightly. If they don't close, they're not fresh and probably dead, meaning they're not suitable for cooking or eating. You can buy scallops that have been shucked (opened) but make sure they look plump and moist.

Even though they may not look very lively, fresh shellfish are indeed alive and need to breathe. Sealing them in a plastic bag will smother them, so be sure to poke numerous holes in the bag with a wooden skewer or better still, keep them on ice. Place the shellfish in a bowl half filled with crushed ice, then cover with a wet, clean towel. Put a bit more ice on top of the towel to keep it moist and place the bowl in the coldest part of your fridge. Drain off any meltwater that collects in the bowl and use within a day or two.

Preparation

With a stiff brush, give your clams, mussels, scallops or oysters a good scrub under cold running water. If any barnacles are growing on the shells, scrape them away with another shell and remove the tangled "beard" from mussels. If any shells remain open after a light tap, discard them.

To shuck clams:

1. Place the clams on a baking sheet on in the freezer for 5-10 minutes, so that the meat loosens from the shells a bit.

2. Hold the shell so that the hinge is against the palm of your hand and insert the edge of an oyster shucker's knife, or a dull kitchen knife, between the top and bottom shells.

3. Slide the blade all around the shell so that you cut right through the hinge, opening the shell.

4. Slip the knife edge between the meat and the shell to remove.

To shuck oysters:

1. Place the oyster flat-side up on a chopping board or non-slip work surface. Firmly grip the oyster with a tea towel, or wear a shucker's glove, and leave the hinged end exposed.

2. Place the tip of your oyster knife between the two shells, on either side of the hinge. Applying firm but gentle pressure, press inward. Twist and wiggle the knife tip with gentle pressure until the blade has made its way inside.

3. Continue to twist and press the knife in until the top shell pops open. Try to retain the flavourful oyster liquor by keeping the shell level as you shuck.

4. Clean any grit from your knife, then pry the shell open by inserting the knife tip in a couple of more spots, twisting it to release the shell completely. Run the knife edge along the inside of the upper shell to cut the muscle attaching it to the top shell.

5. Run the knife edge along the inside of the lower shell, and gently cut the oyster free. Leave in the half shell until ready to use, or to serve raw, transfer the oyster in the bottom shell to a bed of crushed ice to keep it level, retaining the juices, and serve immediately.

To shuck scallops:

1. Follow the method above as shucking a scallop is very similar to shucking an oyster. Slide the knife in between the top and bottom shells of the scallop near the hinge.

2. Follow the inside of the shell with the knife to release the scallop from that side of the shell, enabling you to remove the top.

3. Inside the scallop will have a covering called a frill and a black sack which is the gut. Either use the knife to cut this away or pull it away with your fingers.

4. This should leave the white meat and the orange coral. Some people like the coral and some people just prefer to eat the white meat so it is entirely up to you whether you keep this part. Rinse the scallop to get rid of any grit and then it will be ready for you to cook.

Your shellfish can now be steamed, grilled, baked or stewed (such as in bouillabaisse) according to your preference or the recipe you want to follow. Enjoy!

Handy Hints

· Mussels and oysters are farmed in the UK and, in some cases, it is possible to buy directly from the farms.

· Prawns bought in supermarkets will almost always have been frozen first. It is important to be aware of this as, in some cases, you will not be able to refreeze them.

· Go for prawns from cold waters like the Atlantic rather than warm water prawns from Asia as they have far more flavour.

· Buying live shellfish directly from the people catching it or farming it is the best way to guarantee its freshness.

Common Types of Fish and How to Cook Them

Proper Preparation

Rinse fresh fish under very cold water to remove surface bacteria, then pat dry with kitchen roll or a clean tea towel. Unless you're cooking it straight away, wrap the cleaned and dried fish in reusable wax paper or cling film to minimize oxygen exposure, then store in the fridge on crushed ice.

Cooking Tips

Fish has a reputation for being difficult to cook, but if you time things carefully it doesn't have to be a daunting task. Overcooked fish does become very dry, which affects the flavour and texture. It becomes overcooked more quickly than meat, because the proteins in fish muscles are designed for cold temperatures and can start to coagulate at room temperature. Most fish dries out around 60°c and the flesh is fragile because it's low in collagen, meaning fish sticks to pans and baking trays more easily, so bear that in mind when cooking your fish.

Fatty Fish

Fish in general are lean animals, but so-called fatty fish are about 5% or more fat by weight. Because of this quality, they can stand up to dry-heat cooking methods such as sautéing or grilling. Fat content varies by species and even the location of a fillet, but in general, farmed fish are fattier than wild-caught fish.

1. Carp is a freshwater fish with coarse, tough flesh and lots of bones. Since fish bones are smaller and have less calcium than those of other animals, they can soften (and even dissolve) with cooking. Carp is commonly poached or steamed whole in Chinese dishes, although Sichuan-style whole carp is fried in a wok with Shaoxing wine, soy sauce, spring onions, ginger, star anise, dried hot chillies, and Sichuan peppercorns. In Eastern European Jewish cuisine, it's made into gefilte fish or poached with sweet and sour sauce.

2. Chilean Sea Bass (aka Patagonian toothfish) isn't actually part of the bass family. It has firm, white flesh that produces thick flakes with a rich flavour and is around 14% fat by weight. Chilean sea bass average 7 to 18 kilograms but can weigh up to 45! Try pan-searing this substantial fish for crispy skin, served with fresh seasonal greens.

3. Salmon is popular both for its versatility in the kitchen and the fact that it's packed with nutrients such as Omega 3 fatty acids. Born in freshwater, salmon migrate to saltwater and return to their home rivers to spawn. Salmon has a tender texture and mild-to-rich flavour, depending on the species and whether it's farm raised or wild caught. Farmed salmon tend to be fattier, while wild salmon tend to have more flavour and firmer flesh.

Lean Fish

Most fish are considered lean, meaning they're less than 5% fat by weight, and tend to benefit from wet cooking methods (such as steaming or poaching) and rich or creamy sauces.

1. Bass can refer to hundreds of different species that all tend to have firm, mild-tasting flesh and simple skeletons that are good for filleting. Their low collagen content can lead to bass tasting dry, but leaving the skin on and cooking the fish whole results in a crispy exterior and incredibly moist flesh.

2. Trout are typically freshwater fish. Although related to salmon, trout don't have the same pink flesh because their diets are different. The exception is steelhead trout, which eat the same crustaceans that give salmon their pigment. Rainbow trout are the most commonly available variety, often sold whole due to their small size. They have a slightly nutty flavour and delicate texture and are available year-round. Arctic char, a type of trout farmed in Iceland and Canada, can have just as much fat as salmon.

3. Tuna's high myoglobin content gives its raw flesh a deep red colour and meaty flavour. Tuna is best cooked to around 48-50°c when the flesh is not quite opaque, as it is delicate with very little fat. Try encrusting a tuna steak with sesame seeds to protect the meat and add a nutty flavour while searing. This only takes 30 seconds on each side over a medium heat. If the pan gets too hot, add a touch of cold oil to keep the sesame seeds from burning.

4. Cod are saltwater fish that can be found from the Atlantic to the Pacific. Both varieties are mild in flavour with flaky white flesh. Atlantic cod has less moisture, a firmer texture and sweeter flavour than Pacific cod.

5. Halibut is the largest of the flatfish, a type of sideways-swimming fish with both eyes on one side of the head. It has firm white flesh with more collagen than other fish, so it's more forgiving in terms of dryness. Found in the North Atlantic and northern Pacific, halibut can be very large so it's commonly sold as frozen (or previously frozen) fillets. Try pan seared halibut with brown butter and sage.

6. Monkfish (aka anglerfish) averages 3 to 6 kilograms, a good proportion of which is boneless, dense tail meat typically sold as skinned fillets, since the skin can make monkfish taste tough when cooked. It has a sweet flavour and firm texture that's often compared to lobster or scallops.

7. Swordfish are distinguished by the 'swords' or bills that stick out from their upper jaws, which they use to slash at prey. These large fish (averaging 20 to 90 kilograms) have dense, meaty, almost boneless flesh that can be white or pink. Try pan roasting swordfish steaks in butter.

SOURCE: https://www.masterclass.com/articles/19-different-types-of-fish-for-eating-and-cooking-learn-how-to-eat-fish-sustainably#15-types-of-lean-fish

Saltwater in His Veins

A formative childhood by the sea helped lay the foundations for Mike Warner's lifelong passion for seafood.

A PASSION FOR SEAFOOD
Fish Shop open Tues – Sat at Grange Farm Shop, Hasketon IP136HN

Website: www.apassionfor seafood.com

Instagram and Facebook @apassion forseafood

Twitter @PassionSeafood

Artisan fish sellers, supplying seasonal British fish and shellfish direct from UK day boats to London fishmongers and chefs.

Middle right and bottom middle photos: Tobias Warner

Growing up in a seaside Suffolk community, many happy days in Mike's youth were spent fishing, potting for lobster and crewing for local fishermen. The saltwater flowing through his veins has driven him to dedicate much of his life to promoting coastal culture in both work and leisure: catching, eating, sourcing, advising, selling, and writing about seafood. Ten years ago, he began channelling his love for the fishing industry into a blog, A Passion for Seafood, which was twice shortlisted for the prestigious Guild of Food Writers Awards. This developed into a writing career taking him to a vast number of ports and harbours across the UK, spending invaluable time with fishermen across the country and connecting them with consumers by telling their stories. A move into consultancy came next; the countless hours spent at sea and working in bustling harbours, quays and fish markets were put to good use on projects promoting British seafood and its native fishing communities. This continued until the arrival of the pandemic in 2020 forced Mike to change tack once more.

"I knew I had to reinvent myself again, so I started working with fishermen here in Suffolk, whose market had effectively closed, and I used contacts in retail and hospitality to help sell their wild bass and lobsters to London-based fishmongers during the lockdown. Then the restaurants came back online and we eventually established a wholesale business buying from boats all around the UK, bringing all the produce into Suffolk and delivering it to London."

So, from the wild shores of the Suffolk Heritage Coast to Portland Bill, the quintessential Cornish fishing villages of Looe and Mevagissey to westerly Newlyn, North'ards to the Scottish West and East Coasts, and then south again to Northumberland, A Passion for Seafood provides the finest in seasonal species, landed, iced and with clients within 48 hours. Lobsters, bass, crabs, langoustines, hand-dived scallops – it's all provided with a commitment to total traceability, sustainability and, as ever, with the passion and real-life stories behind the catch promoted throughout.

Mike particularly enjoys working with restaurants in his beloved home county of Suffolk, partnering with local chefs to showcase seasonality on their menus and providing these local establishments with fresh fish, sometimes just hours out of the water. In October 2020, the opportunity came up to run a pop-up fishmonger at a local farm shop and Mike took the plunge, which eventually led to a permanent fish shop where loyal customers queue five days a week for the artisanal seafood on offer. Despite a hectic couple of years, Mike's ingrained passion for seafood is burning brighter than ever and he's always looking for fresh ways to indulge it.

"It feels a bit like I've come full circle, being back in Suffolk and basing my life around seafood. They call it the sigh of the sea: once it beckons you, you'll always find yourself returning to it. I think the next step will be an oyster bar or a seafood café, perhaps, so we can continue bringing those all-important stories behind the seafood to the consumer."

A Passion For Seafood
Pulled Skate & Paprika Potato Cakes

I prefer my skate cooked simply in brown butter with capers or with cockles or brown shrimps, but this recipe is great for children and introduces them to a different species without the fuss of having to eat straight off the bone.

PREPARATION TIME: 15 MINUTES | COOKING TIME: 40 MINUTES | SERVES 4

METHOD

Poach the wing in a pan of salted water with the black peppercorns and bay leaves for 8 minutes. Once poached, ladle out and drain. Fork the ray meat away from the wing and set aside.

Boil the potatoes until they are soft and then mash, incorporating the mustard, crème fraiche and 100g of salted butter. Season with salt and pepper.

Put the mix in a large bowl and fork in the ray meat, adding the cheddar, paprika, chives and spring onion. Work everything together and add as much egg as is necessary to bind, taking care not to drown the mixture.

Mould the mix into 8 cakes (approximately one tablespoon each) and flatten slightly, ready for frying.

Melt the remaining 100g of salter butter in a heavy frying pan and introduce the cakes when it starts to foam. Fry the cakes, turning once or twice until both sides are crispy and golden brown.

Repeat this with the remaining cakes so the pan isn't overcrowded and then serve with a green salad.

INGREDIENTS

500g Thornback Ray wing, skinned
A few black peppercorns
2 bay leaves
500g floury potatoes
1 tsp English mustard
2 tbsp crème fraiche
200g salted butter
Sea salt
Ground black pepper
2 handfuls of mature cheddar, grated
1 tbsp smoked paprika
Small bunch of chives, finely chopped
4 spring onions, finely chopped
1 free-range egg, beaten

"They call it the sigh of the sea: once it beckons you, you'll always find yourself returning to it."

A Passion For Seafood's Mike Warner

ADAM'S

Star Studded

Adam's restaurant, run by Adam and Natasha Stokes, is a Michelin-starred restaurant in Birmingham, offering an à la carte menu alongside a signature tasting menu focused on and built around the best British produce.

ADAM'S
16 Waterloo Street
Birmingham
B2 5UG

Telephone:
0121 643 3745

Website:
www.adamsrestaurant.co.uk

Adam's is a contemporary British fine dining Michelin-starred restaurant in the heart of Birmingham, serving modern dishes with a world class wine list.

When looking for the ideal place to launch, Adam and Natasha wanted to find a thriving environment where they could allow their creativity to flourish. They eventually settled on Birmingham, recognising the city as a progressive and forward-thinking environment for restaurateurs.

Within six months of opening their doors in the city back in 2013, the pair had led Adam's to a Michelin star, becoming only the fourth restaurant in Birmingham with this recognition, while three AA rosettes followed shortly after.

On his approach to running a restaurant and Adam's particular style, founder Adam Stokes said: "My aim is not to baffle, but to excite and enthuse guests with the accurate cooking of quality ingredients served in an approachable environment."

Midlands-born head chef James Goodyear now heads up the award-winning kitchen after joining the Adam's team in 2021. With one, two and three Michelin-starred experience both in the UK and abroad, James brings an exciting collaboration of classical training and gastronomic delights to Adam's.

On taking on the role, James said: "I can't wait to get started, there's so much potential here to take Adam's to the next level. The young team of chefs are great, very hungry and enthusiastic. My culinary style is built around modern, European fine dining, so Adam's is a great fit for me. The kitchen has everything a chef could dream of and it's very clear that it has been designed by someone who loves to produce quality food. I'm also thrilled to be working with Adam Stokes; having someone like him to collaborate with and run ideas by will be brilliant."

Adam's holds a string of accolades including a Michelin star, three AA Rosettes and appears in the top 50 UK restaurants in the Good Food Guide. The restaurant was awarded a Travellers' Choice Award in 2021 for the eighth consecutive year and was named the Number 4 Restaurant in the UK and 18 in Europe on TripAdvisor.

Adam's has continued to evolve in the years since and is now firmly established as one of Birmingham's most popular restaurants.

Adam's
Cured Bream in a Caramelised Cream and Kelp Reduction

We recommend using the freshest possible sustainable UK fish available, allowing the main ingredient to really shine with a punch of savoury umami to bring it to life. The key is good preparation of the bream and using the freshest fish available.

PREPARATION TIME: 2 HOURS 30 MINUTES | COOKING TIME: 2 HOURS 10 MINUTES | SERVES 8 – 10

INGREDIENTS
250g pearl barley
25g kelp
500g chestnut mushrooms, thinly sliced
25g malt extract
2g soy sauce
2g dashi vinegar
1g xanthan gum
250g extra virgin rapeseed oil
100g ginger, finely chopped
1 mooli
100g pine nuts
2 x 500ml double cream
50g white miso
1 large leek
Wakame seaweed powder
Shiso leaf
Allysum/chive flowers

For the pickled seaweed
500g fresh red dulse seaweed
100g chardonnay vinegar
100g rice wine vinegar
50g sugar
50ml water
Pinch of salt

For the bream
4 large bream fillets
1kg Maldon salt
1kg Demerara sugar
Pinch of yuzu powder

METHOD
For the mushroom dressing
Place the barley on one tray and the kelp on another. Roast the kelp for 5 minutes and the barley for 10 minutes, both at 160°c. Place the barley, kelp and chestnut mushrooms in a pan with 500ml of water and simmer at 80°c for 2 hours, then strain. Weigh the liquid and then reduce by one third. Blend in the malt extract, soy sauce, dashi vinegar and xanthan gum then chill in the fridge.

For the ginger oil, pickled seaweed and bream
Place the rapeseed oil and ginger in a pan and cook at 70°c for 2 hours, then strain. Mix all of the ingredients for the pickled seaweed together in a container or jar and leave to pickle. Strain after 2 hours.
Skin the bream fillets and cure for 30 minutes in the salt, sugar and yuzu mixture. Wash the cure off, dry the fillets and then thinly slice. Arrange the fish into discs of four slices and store between squares of greaseproof paper.

For the pickled mooli discs and toasted pine nuts
Thinly slice and cut out small mooli discs before covering with Asian pickle. Strain after 30 minutes. Dry toast the pine nuts on a flat tray at 170°c for approximately 8 minutes. Once cooled, finely chop half of the toasted nuts.

For the caramelised cream and crispy leek
Place the two measures of double cream in separate pans to reduce. Once reduced by half, remove one pan from the heat. Keep reducing the other until it splits and caramelises. Strain the solids then whisk the cream, white miso and chopped toasted pine nuts together, seasoning with salt to taste. Thinly slice the leek and deep fry at 160°c until crispy. Drain on kitchen paper and season lightly with salt.

To assemble
Place a spoonful of caramelised cream on the bottom of the plate and top with the sliced portioned bream, creating a neat circle. Glaze with the ginger oil. Place five whole pine nuts, some pickled seaweed and mooli on top of the bream. Neatly rest the crispy leek on top and dust with seaweed powder. Top with the shiso leaf and flowers then spoon the mushroom dressing around the bream and split with a small amount of ginger oil.

"My aim is not to baffle, but to excite and enthuse..."

Adam Stokes, Adam's and The Oyster Club

BATTLEFIELD REST

Southside Special

A family-run continental restaurant with a strong Italian spirit and a Glaswegian heart.

Built as a particularly exotic looking tram station in 1915, this Southside landmark fell into a state of disrepair before being rescued in a restoration led by Marco Giannasi, who opened an Italian bistro here in 1994. He bought the building from the council for one pound and spent two years meticulously creating what has become a much-loved local restaurant. The interiors are sophisticated and gloriously traditional. The rooms seem bigger on the inside than they do on the outside. It's like taking a step into a self-contained Glasgow culinary bubble where service is prompt and warm, conversation flows as easily as the wine, people relax and linger over their meal.

You'll find familiar pasta Bolognese, carbonara or arrabbiata while signature dishes include a linguine frutti di mare: a seafood blend of West Coast mussels, prawns, Fort William farmed salmon, squid sautéed with fennel, chilli and garlic white wine sauce. Marino, the former head chef, is still with the restaurant after almost 28 years and has stepped back to let Mark Donnelly – another longstanding team member with 12 years under his belt – take his place. Manager Tony has also been at Battlefield Rest since its opening: "they were there for the beginning of the story," owner Marco says with a smile.

The redevelopment of the old Victoria hospital site beside Battlefield Rest will bring new people to the area, but Marco says he still sees the same customers coming year after year. There's a consistency to the cooking and some enduring dishes on the menu but they like to play around with things in the kitchen too. Experiments like their haggis cannelloni proved popular. "We like to source the best Scottish produce, and I also independently buy pasta products, prosciutto and salami from the North of Tuscany," Marco explains. "My family has roots in Tuscany so I like to keep that connection. You can have the best of Scotland and the best of Tuscany in the Southside of Glasgow. Customers appreciate we are trying to do new things and pick up new ingredients to keep the menu alive."

Marco says he now sees customers who started coming to Battlefield Rest as children returning as adults with their own children. "They come back now they are big boys and girls. The restaurant still has a charm for them. They bring their families. We have that kind of relationship with customers, it's an emotional connection that makes the restaurant special, beyond the meal and the atmosphere. They leave their troubles at the door and talk to us, we counsel them and they counsel us. It's that kind of place."

BATTLEFIELD REST
55 Battlefield Road
Glasgow
G42 9GL

Telephone: 0141 636 6955

Website: battlefieldrest.co.uk

Eye-catching building for a continental bistro with a balance of Italian and Scottish flavours.

Battlefield Rest
Smoked Haddock Risotto with Stornoway Black Pudding & Crispy Egg

A dish that matches the character of Battlefield Rest, this risotto is ideal for sharing with friends. Bring the flavours of the Southside's favourite Italian bistro to your own kitchen with this simple yet stunning recipe.

PREPARATION TIME: 20 MINUTES | COOKING TIME: 25 MINUTES | SERVES 4

INGREDIENTS

For the risotto
50g butter
1 onion, chopped
1 clove of garlic, chopped
250g Arborio risotto rice
50ml dry white wine
1 litre fish stock
2 leeks, finely sliced
300g smoked haddock
50g parmesan, freshly grated
Salt and pepper

For the crispy egg
4 free-range eggs
50g flour
1 egg, beaten
100g panko breadcrumbs

For the black pudding
4 slices of Stornoway black pudding

For the garnish
50g rocket
Drizzle of olive oil

METHOD

For the risotto
Heat the butter in a heavy-based saucepan, then add the onion and garlic. Fry gently until the onion softens and goes transparent. Add all the rice, mixing well with the butter, onion and garlic, then fry while stirring for 45 seconds. Add the white wine and stir for a further 30 seconds, then add the fish stock. Bring your risotto to the boil and cook for 5 minutes, stirring all the time, then turn the heat down to a simmer for a further 10 minutes, while continuing to stir. Add the leeks and smoked haddock to the risotto mix and gently cook for 5 more minutes until the rice is cooked through. Season with salt and pepper, then add the parmesan and take off the heat.

For the crispy egg
Boil the eggs for 5 minutes and 30 seconds, then cool them down and take off their shells. Dip the egg in flour, then in the beaten egg, then the breadcrumbs and set aside. Deep fry the egg for 1 minute then season with salt while hot.

For the black pudding
Place the black pudding slices under a preheated grill and cook for 3 minutes on each side.

To serve
Time to bring it all together. Place a slice of black pudding on a plate. Spoon some risotto onto the black pudding and then place a small bunch of rocket on the pile. Cut the egg in half and then place on top. Drizzle with olive oil and serve.

"It's an emotional connection that makes the restaurant special."

Marco Grannasi, Battlefield Rest

THE BEAR INN

We're Going On A Bear Hunt

First established as a coaching inn in the 16th century, the Bear Inn underwent a significant renovation before reopening its doors in August 2021. Less than a year later, the accolades continue to stack up for this Shropshire gem.

THE BEAR INN
Drayton Road
Hodnet
TF9 3NH

Telephone: 01630 685214

Website: www.thebearinnhodnet.com

Completely renovated in 2021, this country inn within the Shropshire village of Hodnet boasts 12 luxury bedrooms, a bar, restaurant and courtyard dining.

From two well-deserved AA rosettes to the building's five-star accommodation being listed by The Times as one of the best places to stay in the UK, you can say it's been a whirlwind start for Mel and Martin Board, the dynamic husband-and-wife duo who operate the venue situated in the charming rural village of Hodnet.

A stylish renovation, headed by leading UK interior designer Octavia Dickinson, has worked wonders in blending the venue's rich history with timeless refinement and comfort. The timber frame architecture, flickering fires and low ceilings remain, now combined with colourful, folk-inspired décor, inviting bedrooms and plenty of contemporary luxuries to bring the elegant experience right up to date.

It's rare that a building survives for over two centuries without some interesting tales to tell, and the Bear is no different in that respect. Beneath the ground, its ancient tunnels and cellars hid rebellious monks from church officials and provided tax-free smuggling routes for thrifty publicans. Its fabled bear pit was revived in the 1970s when the publican – for a time – installed two real grizzlies, Madge and Bib, who were later donated to Newquay Zoo.

Back to the modern day and sustainability is very much at the heart of the ethos here, from the strictly seasonal menu of modern British food right down to the ground source heating warming the pub. For maximum freshness and traceability, they grow ingredients in the 200-year-old walled garden at Hodnet Hall (the building itself is in fact owned by the Hodnet Estate), and anything that can't be plucked from their kitchen garden they will aim to source locally. Naturally, you'll also find a few choice ales from Shropshire-based brewers on tap.

Fittingly, the village of Hodnet takes its name from the old Welsh hawdd nant, meaning peaceful valley. Pay them a visit and enjoy this recently revived haven of stunning food, drink and hospitality for yourself.

All pictures except top left and middle left: Andy Hughes

The Bear Inn

Pan Fried Stonebass, Potato and Leek

This is a light, flavoursome, springtime dish, one of my favourites.When cooking the stonebass, get the pan red hot before putting the fish in, then take it off the heat until the fish relaxes, place back on the heat, add butter and baste until golden.

PREPARATION TIME: 1 HOUR | COOKING TIME: 2 HOURS | SERVES 4

METHOD

Prepare the stonebass by cutting into 200g portions. Peel the potatoes and cut the top and bottom so each one sits flat, then press into rings with a cutter. Place them in a baking tray, add 100g of the butter and just enough water to sit under them, then cook In the oven at 180°c for 50 minutes, shaking every 10 minutes until golden brown.

Cut 1 leek into 5cm fondants for cooking later. For the sweet and sour leeks, cut the other leek into a manageable size and then halve lengthways. Take the core out, finely slice horizontally and place in a tub. Bring the ginger beer, white wine vinegar, water and sugar up the boil and pour over sliced leeks while still warm.

For the dill oil, blanch the dill for 10 seconds, refresh in iced water, dry thoroughly, then add to a blender with 100ml of vegetable oil and blend for 5 minutes. Slightly dampen a clean cloth with a bit of oil and put this inside a sieve over a jug. Pour in the dill oil and leave to pass out the pulp.

Slice the shallots and garlic, sauté on a medium heat without colouring them for 2 minutes, then add the white wine and reduce by half. Pass the mixture through a sieve into a clean pan and put the liquor back on the stove on a low heat. Dice the 200g of cold butter into small cubes and add them slowly into the wine reduction, whisking until each cube has emulsified into the sauce.

Get a frying pan red hot with a splash of oil, season the stonebass skin and add to the hot pan, carefully laying the fish away from yourself. Pull the pan off the heat and wait until the fish relaxes (roughly 90 seconds). Put the pan back on a medium heat and add 100g of butter. Wait until the butter starts to go nutty and golden brown in colour and then baste the fish. Cook it for 2 minutes skin side down, then flip and take off the heat and leave to rest in the pan. Add a squeeze of lemon juice and remove after 1 minute, placing the fish onto a tray. Put this pan back on the heat and add the leek fondants. Cook on one side for 3 minutes on a medium heat, then add the samphire and cook for a further 2 minutes.

To plate, add the leeks, potato and samphire to the bowl, place the stonebass on top and add a squeeze of dill oil to the sauce, then pour around the side of the bowl.

INGREDIENTS

2 medium sides of stonebass
2 large potatoes
500g butter (keep 200g cold for sauce)
2 leeks
100ml ginger beer
100ml white wine vinegar
100ml water
100g sugar
1 bunch of fresh dill
100ml vegetable oil
2 shallots
2 cloves of garlic
100g samphire
200ml white wine

"Sustainability is very much at the heart of the ethos."

The Bear Inn at Hornet

A Great Catch

A setting that oozes charm and was once described by William Morris as "the most beautiful village in England," Bibury is also home to one of the most sustainable trout farms in the country.

BIBURY TROUT FARM
Bibury
Cirencester
Gloucestershire
GL7 5NL

Telephone:
01285 740215/2

Website: www.
biburytroutfarm.
co.uk

One of the oldest trout farms in the country, open to visitors, producing top quality rainbow and brown trout for both the restocking and table markets.

Smatterings of ancient and picturesque buildings make up Bibury, with nearby Arlington Mill and Row mentioned in the Doomsday Book, no less. However it's not just the village that draws visitors these days; Bibury Trout Farm prides itself on offering year-round supplies of their nationally recognised brand of trout.

With a low-intensity approach, they only allow 10kg per cubic metre, meaning the fish have plenty of room, growing to a healthy size with beautiful fins and tails. Reared in excellent conditions, the freshness is second to none as trout can be taken home on the very same day they are caught.

While the main purpose of the farm is to restock rivers, reservoirs and lakes up and down the UK, it's also an immersive tourist attraction, with visitors coming to enjoy the attractive grounds, feed the fish and even catch their own.

"It's all about the experience of catching it yourself," says owner Kate Marriott. "Some inner city children come and visit, and many have never seen a live fish before. The hunter-gatherer aspect is what makes it exciting for them."

If you're more into eating than catching fish, then the café is the best place to sample their wares in the summer. As well as doing all their own smoking and processing, they freshly make fishcakes, quiches, pâté and much more besides. You can also buy their range of freshly caught fish to take away with you.

A family affair, the farm is run by husband and wife partnership Kate Marriott and Terry Allen, while Kate's sister Sheena takes care of the retail side of things. Loyal and passionate, most of their other staff have been there just as long as the family, providing unrivalled expertise in the industry.

From supplying local restaurants, markets and wholesalers, to rearing their own eggs (Bibury are one of the few farms that can breed trout) and smoking fish in their small in-house kiln, the team work hard to ensure Bibury Trout continues its legacy. Look out for their name on the menu the next time you're dining out!

Picture top right and middle left: Kay Ransom Photography

Bibury Trout Farm Smoked Trout Fishcakes

Trout is packed full of flavour and this recipe is super quick and easy to make, perfect for a midweek dinner.

PREPARATION TIME: 15 MINUTES | COOKING TIME: 45 MINUTES | SERVES 2

METHOD

To make the fishcakes, boil the potatoes for 30 minutes or until tender. Drain the potatoes and then mash lightly.

Add the smoked trout to the mashed potato and mix in gently. Fold in the parsley and dill, add some fresh lemon juice to taste, then season with salt and pepper. Allow the mixture to cool until almost cold.

Shape the trout mixture into 4 fishcakes. Whisk the eggs in a shallow bowl and put the flour and breadcrumbs into separate bowls. Dip the fishcakes in the flour, the egg and then the breadcrumbs to coat. Reshape if necessary.

To cook the fishcakes, place a frying pan over a medium heat and add enough oil to come about 3mm up the side. Once the oil is hot, fry the cakes for approximately 3–4 minutes on each side. Remove and drain on kitchen paper to soak up excess oil before serving.

INGREDIENTS

200g potatoes
200g smoked trout
30g flat leaf parsley
30g dill
1 lemon
2 eggs
100g plain flour
200g breadcrumbs
Salt and black pepper
Oil, for frying

"It's all about the experience of catching it yourself."

Kate Marriott, Bibury Trout Farm

THE BUTTERY

Spreading The Word

With a classic approach to drinking and dining, The Buttery demonstrates the best standards of Glasgow hospitality.

Ryan James bought Two Fat Ladies on Dumbarton Road and then took over The Buttery twelve years ago when the group was in the process of expansion. At the time, they opted for calling their newest unit Two Fat Ladies at The Buttery. Yet, as the years have gone-by the management team decided it was time for the building to return to its roots and has gone back, at least in name, to its first incarnation.

THE BUTTERY
652 Argyle Street
Glasgow
G3 8UF

Telephone: 0141
221 8188

Website:
twofatladies
restaurant.com

Landmark
Glasgow
restaurant
with acclaimed
seafood menu.

The Buttery has been around for quite some time– the building dates from 1870 – and boasts a wealth of history and stories from patrons who have been visiting throughout the decades. On one level, it's an old-school classic, but it could also be considered something of a hipster trendsetter as, it's fair to say, The Buttery liked Finnieston before it was cool. This is the type of place that is difficult to create: it has to evolve over time. The oak and mahogany, the plush bar and reception area, tartan carpet, stained glass. You are entering a time capsule of Glasgow hospitality that also possesses innovation in the kitchen. It is a traditional dining room without being stuffy. If you took a date here, they would be impressed without being overawed. The staff glide between tables and put guests at ease. There's a buzz of easy conversation.

The Buttery sources ingredients from across Scotland, Ryan explains: "Most of the fish that we use is landed at Peterhead and comes down to Glasgow. We're all fighting for the best of that produce to a certain extent, but there's certainly a plentiful supply of fish. There's also great beef, very good game as well, especially from Ayrshire."

The job of the kitchen is to make these ingredients shine and to ensure customers have a good time and leave well fed. Ryan continues: "We let the flavours speak for themselves to a certain extent. I'm not looking to educate people or teach them new things about food, I just want to serve up the best dishes at a fair price. "I think people should be very proud when they talk about Scotland's larder. Sometimes we don't say that loud enough. We find visitors are totally impressed with how good the food is in Glasgow."

Ryan attributes one key ingredient to the restaurant's current standing and success: "It is all about the staff. We've been fortunate to have a fantastic team, both front and back, throughout the years. For me, hospitality is all about warmth and generosity and that's what we look for in our brigade and something I believe we do well. The last couple of years has emphasised how important hospitality is as a profession."

The Buttery

West Coast Scallops, Golden Raisin Purée, Spiced Cauliflower Fritters

We found that the fresh scallops worked well with the earthy tones of mildly spiced cauliflower, while the raisin and saffron purée adds a touch of both sweetness and elegance.

PREPARATION TIME: 5 MINUTES | COOKING TIME: 10 MINUTES | SERVES 1-2

METHOD

For the golden raisin purée
Place all the ingredients into a saucepan and add enough water to cover the raisins. Bring to the boil and then simmer until soft. Remove from the heat and use a hand blender to purée the mixture. Pass the purée through a fine sieve, pushing it down with the back of a ladle. Season to taste and then set aside.

For the cauliflower fritters
Mix all the dry ingredients together in a bowl and whisk in 250-350ml of water until you have a batter consistency. Break or cut the cauliflower into florets, then cut them in half. Preheat a deep fat fryer to 165°c. Dip the florets in the batter and place one at a time into the fryer with enough room for the florets to be moved about while cooking. When lightly coloured, take the fritters out and place them on paper towels to drain.

For the scallops
Preheat a frying pan with a little oil in. Season the scallops and then place them into the pan. Check after 30 seconds to see if they've coloured nicely. When golden brown, turn over and repeat the cooking process. Finish the scallops by adding a splash of lemon juice, rolling it around the pan to deglaze and then removing the scallops from the heat.

To serve
Warm the raisin purée and create a large tear drop shape with it on the serving plate, using the back of a spoon. Deep fry the cauliflower fritters again, removing and draining them when golden brown. Place the hot scallops and fritters on the plate with a pea shoot salad, fresh tomato and a few leaves of lemon balm to garnish.

INGREDIENTS

For the golden raisin purée
100g golden raisins
25ml white wine
1 shallot, diced
A pinch of saffron

For the cauliflower fritters
100g self-raising flour
100g cornflour
15g mild madras curry powder
1 cauliflower

For the scallops
2 scallops
1 lemon, juiced

To serve
Pea shoots
Fresh tomato
Lemon balm leaves

"A time capsule of Glasgow hospitality that also possesses innovation in the kitchen."

The Buttery

The Italian Dodd

Dodds Restaurant has been a staple of Ambleside for many decades, and has built up a reputation for a great atmosphere with food and drink that keeps locals coming back for more.

DODDS RESTAURANT
Rydal Road
Ambleside
Cumbria
LA22 9AN

Telephone:
015394 32134

Website:
www.
doddsrestaurant.
co.uk

Friendly Ambleside restaurant open for lunch and evening meals from a menu of Italian-inspired dishes.

Laszlo and Tamas had dreamt of having their own restaurant since their teenage years, so they felt very lucky to have the opportunity of taking on Dodds Restaurant in 2008 with the support of their previous employer. They felt that the right thing to do was to keep the name, carrying on the legacy of the original owner, M.R. Dodds, while bringing the restaurant up to date. This is reflected today in the modern yet cosy dining area and the food served straight from the open kitchen.

They aim for Dodds to stand out from the crowd, as well as to provide a friendly and approachable service thanks to the close-knit team. The menus are filled with wonderful dishes influenced by the flavours of the Mediterranean and seasonal availability. The focus is on Italian cuisine, as head chef Laszlo enjoys what he calls the "never ending source of ideas and inspiration" from the wide regional variety it offers. Tamas, who looks after front of house, also likes to experiment in the bar with new drinks pairings and he personally chooses the best wines to go with the flavourful food. His team also put a lot of effort into turning locally roasted beans into the smoothest coffee experiences for their guests.

Laszlo often tries out new ideas on the specials menu, as "it's a good way to gauge interest and feedback from the customers." The style of food served at Dodds has led to close relationships with local producers and suppliers, as well as with those across many borders to enable the team to find the best and most unique Italian ingredients and wines. Laszlo sources a wide range of products from cheese to handcrafted cured meats from a small supplier based on the island of Sardinia, where every member of the family has a hands-on role!

Laszlo and Tamas agree that "Dodds' biggest accolade is that we have an ever-growing customer base and the thumbs up from our happy customers." The two say that it's always nice to look back to their younger selves, who would be going out for a few drinks after a hard day in the restaurant, when they're now running home to see their kids! The duo and their team have worked hard to create a place to eat out that's easy going and a joy to revisit; the bubbly atmosphere filled with the chatter of contented guests is all you need to hear to know they've succeeded.

Dodds Restaurant Italian Seafood Stew

This is a very hearty dish full of flavour and imposing colours. The preparation involves a seafood stock, similar to a bisque but not as heavy and without cream. It's a simple dish so even the most novice cooks can produce a beautifully tasty meal.

PREPARATION TIME: 10 MINUTES | COOKING TIME: 1 HOUR | SERVES 4

INGREDIENTS

For the stock
1 tbsp rapeseed oil
1 large onion, chopped
1 stick of celery, chopped
3 cloves of garlic, crushed
6 large tomatoes, chopped
1 red pepper, chopped
200g white fish
8 langoustines
1 tbsp tomato purée
2 litres water
1 tbsp ground paprika
1 tbsp olive oil

For the stew
4 fillets of sea bass, cubed
16 tiger prawns
1kg cleaned mussels
400g squid
1 carrot, finely chopped
1 fennel, finely chopped
1 tbsp chopped chives
1 tbsp chopped dill

METHOD
Method
For the stock
Put all the ingredients except the water, paprika and olive oil in a large pot and fry until golden. Fill the pot with the water, slightly submerging the ingredients. Bring the stock to a simmer and cook for 40 minutes.

Mix the paprika with the olive oil and pour into the stock, letting the mixture simmer for a further 5 minutes.

Strain the mixture through a fine sieve into another pot, leaving you with a thick stock.

For the stew
Cook the fish, shellfish, squid and finely diced vegetables for 4-5 minutes before adding the stock. Let it heat through befrore stirring in the chopped herbs.

Serve with warm garlic bread and a wedge of lemon.

A Taste of the Sardinian Coast

Found on the ground floor of the heritage-listed Eagle Works building in the bustling Kelham Island area of Sheffield, Domo brings a welcome slice of Sardinian coastal life to the Steel City.

DOMO RESTAURANT
Eagle Works
34-36 Cotton
Mill Walk, Little
Kelham, Sheffield
S3 8DH

Telephone: 0114
3221020

Website:
domorestaurant.
co.uk

Warmly
furnished eatery
with a terrace
showcasing
Sardinian cuisine,
including pizza &
pasta dishes.

Photography:
Ellie Grace

Hailing from Castelsardo, a small Sardinian port town, Domo's head chef and co-owner Raffaelle Busceddu has always experienced seafood as a way of life. The town sits on an idyllic hillside and every morning its inhabitants walk down to the harbour to collect the morning's freshly plucked catch, which Sardinian mamas (and papas) spend all day cooking up. As an adult, Rafa decided to cast his net a little wider and work in the UK's hospitality sector, so when he and partner Sarah Elliot decided to go it alone, opening Domo, it was the perfect opportunity to bring the authentic experience of Castelsardo's love of seafood to the Steel City.

This blending of cultures was beautifully encapsulated when they first opened in 2019, with Raffaele's family, including well known chef uncle Dario, who owns Rocca 'Ja, a restaurant in Castelsardo, descending on Sheffield to help run the place and install some truly traditional Sardinian character from the off. Rafa's family also inspire many of the dishes on its 'from the sea' section of the menu, with Domo's much-loved fish stew paying homage to the humble dish his grandad made him as a boy. The fish for dishes such as this is delivered into the restaurant fresh every day, and is lovingly used to create everything from lobster bruschette, to their incredible grilled fish platters for two, and dishes that are traditional to Castelsardo, such as a unique shredded skate and pecorino cheese dish, which almost certainly won't be found anywhere else in the UK.

Since opening in the summer of 2019, Domo restaurant has become a huge hit - not least because of its 5-7pm aperitivo where punters have been snacking on seafood, pizza, bruschetta and olives whilst washing down post-work pints of Menabrea and Aperol Spritz. Its sunbathed courtyard is perfect for alfresco drinking and dining whilst inside you'll find a spacious restaurant and bar area that is designed in an attractive rustic fashion, adorned with Sardinian masks, handwoven baskets and Mediterranean plants. There's the hustle and bustle of a family-run kitchen in one corner – frenetic, passionate and fervent.

The word Domo means home, and it's clear to see that Sarah and Raffaelle have brought their version of home to the city of Sheffield, with that unique blend of incredible home cooked-style seafood served up in an atmosphere akin to a family meal at nonna's place. Sarah and Rafaelle's own words sum up the restaurant perfectly.

"We pride ourselves on serving up the amazing seafood, drinks and hospitality you would find in our small town of Castelsardo, Sardinia. We want you to experience the real Sardinian way of life. Whether you need coffee on the go, lunch with colleagues, after work drinks, feasts with the family, or cocktails at the weekend, we serve up Sardinian tradition all day long. In Castelsardo our door is always open when there's food on the table. We welcome you to our restaurant like we would our home."

Domo Restaurant

Cassola
"Zu Raffellu"

This fantastically flavoursome and fresh fish stew was my Grandad's favourite dish that he would prepare for the family with fish plucked from the harbour that morning, every time I returned home from the UK to Sardinia.

PREPARATION TIME: 15 MINUTES | COOKING TIME: 2 HOURS 15 MINUTES | SERVES 2

METHOD

In a deep pan, heat a little olive oil and the king prawn heads. Let them cook for 10 minutes on a high flame, then add a good dash of white wine along with the water and fish stock granules. Stir in the tomato purée, roughly chop and add the parsley, then let it cook for 1 hour 45 minutes.

In another pan on a medium-high flame, cook the garlic and all the fish (including the prawns) in a little oil for 5 minutes. Pour in 450ml of the prawn head bisque, then halve and add the cherry tomatoes. Cover with a lid and let it cook for another 10 minutes.

Add fresh basil, chilli, salt and pepper to taste. Toast a couple of slices of Altamura bread, drizzle them with olive oil and use to dip in and mop up the sauce.

INGREDIENTS

Olive oil
6 king prawn heads
Dash of white wine
2 litres water
1 tbsp fish stock granules
1 tbsp tomato purée
1 bunch of parsley
2 cloves of garlic, thinly sliced
80g stone bass
80g halibut
80g sea bream
80g baby squid
6 peeled king prawns
2 whole king prawns
300g cherry tomatoes
Fresh basil leaves
Fresh red chilli, sliced
Salt and pepper

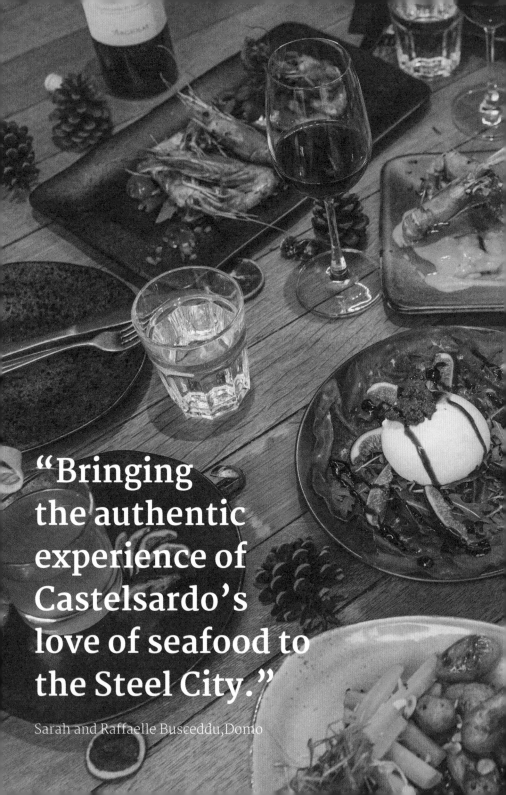

"Bringing the authentic experience of Castelsardo's love of seafood to the Steel City."

Sarah and Raffaelle Busceddu, Domo

Power To The People

The team at The Fish People are united by two things: a passion for seafood and great customer service. They believe that no dish can be better than its ingredients, and that the best ingredients are usually local.

THE FISH PEOPLE
Shields Road
Subway Station,
350 Scotland St,
Glasgow
G5 8QF

Telephone: 0141 429 1609

Website: thefish peopleshop.co.uk

Family-run fishmonger based in Glasgow and serving fresh, high quality seafood to homes and businesses across the UK.

When Andy Bell and family looked at the adjacent industrial café to their southside fishmongers that had lain dormant and disused for many years, they saw an opportunity. Seizing the chance to try something new, they embarked on a substantial renovation of the neighbouring unit. Resplendent in French bistro décor, the doors opened on The Fish People Café in September 2012. For nine wonderful years, the café was a bustling hub for locals, with many loyal and much-loved customers. Sadly, owing to the pandemic, the doors closed in 2020 and the family decided it was time for something new. They launched an at-home delivery service during the first lockdown which quickly proved to be a hit. Fast forward a few years and the company are now delivering fresh fish and seafood meals all over the UK.

The restaurant team was led by head chef John Gillespie, who now operates the 'cook at home' range. He and his team create lots of delicious dishes available from their retail shop and website. John creates a selection of pre-prepared, easy to cook meals, with a weekly special that can be delivered each weekend. John's cooking style consists of simple, classic dishes with an Asian twist, showcased in the tandoori sea bass recipe he has shared in this book. They have repeatedly found this dish to be a customer favourite, almost always selling out. The food philosophy centres on offering high-quality sustainable fish at affordable prices. All fish is sourced from their own fishmongers, they use local suppliers such as Seasonal Produce for their fruit and vegetables, and J.R. Fine Foods for cheese and dairy.

"Our retail shop is next door to the kitchen; we also have a wholesale unit in the East End which supplies Glasgow and the surrounding areas. As a wholesaler we pride ourselves on providing the highest quality of fresh seafood and have a loyal customer base that will testify to this," Laura Bell says. "We're buying the freshest and highest quality produce every day, with a large network of suppliers, mostly within Scotland: places such as Barra, Shetland, Peterhead, though also from the London markets. We never compromise on quality, so if the produce isn't as good as we think it should be, we won't buy it."

The Fish People is a small but dynamic business, changing and adapting as customer habits do. Customers are an eclectic mix of locals, people who travel hours to stock up and visitors to the city. "We are a bit of a destination shop, with an unusual location, so it means all the more when customers travel to see us. Many of the customers are regulars and know the staff well. Teresa and the team ensure that everyone is greeted warmly, and that the high standard of service never slips."

SEABASS
FILLETS
21.50
KILO

WHOLE SPICE
TANDOOR

The Fish People Tandoori Sea Bass

INGREDIENTS

4 whole sea bass (400-450g each)

For the tandoori paste
375g natural yoghurt
10 cloves of garlic, peeled
60g fresh root ginger
5 tbsp sunflower oil
5 tbsp lemon juice
55g paprika
2½ tsp each of garam masala, turmeric, cumin, chilli powder, and salt

For the curry oil
500ml sunflower oil
2 onions, chopped
10 cloves of garlic, chopped
100g root ginger, peeled (keep peelings)
1 cinnamon stick
3 tbsp curry powder
1 tbsp garam masala
1 tbsp ground turmeric
200g tomato purée
500ml extra virgin olive oil
100g fresh coriander
1 tsp salt

For the samphire pakora
100g gram flour
¼ tsp each of crushed coriander seeds, ground cumin, turmeric, chilli powder and salt
Pinch of baking powder
150g samphire

The Fish People offer a modern twist on classic seafood dishes that showcase the finest fresh fish and shellfish that Scotland has to offer.

PREPARATION TIME: 20 MINUTES | COOKING TIME: 20 MINUTES | SERVES 4

METHOD

Ask your fishmonger to gut, scale and score the flesh of the sea bass on each side. This allows the tandoori paste to get into the flesh of the fish. You can make the curry oil and tandoori paste ahead of time as they can be kept in the fridge in sealed containers for 4-6 weeks.

For the tandoori paste
The tandoori paste is very easy to make. Just place all the ingredients into a jug blender or liquidiser and blend until smooth.

For the curry oil
In a heavy-based saucepan, heat the sunflower oil and sweat off the onion, garlic and the finely diced peelings of the root ginger for 5 minutes. Add the cinnamon stick, curry powder, garam masala, and turmeric to cook for a further 2 minutes. Add the tomato purée and olive oil, then simmer at a low heat for 25 minutes, ensuring nothing sticks to the pan, then set aside to cool slightly. After cooling, pass the oil through a mesh sieve and discard all the pulp. Line a sieve with muslin or a J-cloth and place it over a clean bowl. Pour in the oil and let it drip through, then set aside to cool completely. Chop the coriander and blend this and the salt with the curry oil. Finely dice the peeled root ginger and add it to the cooled curry oil.

For the samphire pakora
Mix all the ingredients except the samphire in a bowl and add enough water to make a thick batter. Fold in the samphire and set aside.

For the sea bass
Season the whole bass with salt, fry in a hot pan for 1 minute on each side, then place on a metal oven tray. Spread each fish with a generous amount of tandoori paste and bake in the oven at 220°c for 8-10 minutes.

Meanwhile, place small batches of pakora mix into a deep fat fryer at 180°c for 3-4 minutes until crisp and golden brown. Place a bass on each serving plate, drizzle with the curry oil and place under a hot grill for 1 minute to warm the oil. Serve the cooked fish with the pakora on the side and mini poppadoms, basmati rice and fresh lemon.

SOLE

TROUT
FILLETS
13

PEAT
SMOKED
HADDOCK
16.80 KILO

"We never compromise on quality so if the produce isn't as good as we think it should be, we don't buy it."

Laura, The Fish People

THE FISH SHOP

The Perfect Catch

For the freshest quality seafood at the right price in Bristol and Bath, plus filleting courses and eco-friendly local delivery, The Fish Shop is the place to go.

THE FISH SHOP
143 Gloucester Road
Bristol
BS7 8BA
&
2 Third Avenue
Bath
BA2 3NY

Telephone: 0117 9241988

Website: www. lovethefishshop. co.uk

Specialising in really fresh dayboat fish and seafood from the south coast, with shops in Bath and Bristol stocking a wide range of shellfish, smoked fish, deli products, sauces and frozen seafood.

The Fish Shop specialises in really fresh dayboat fish and seafood from the south coast. There are two locations, Bath and Bristol, which both stock a wide range of shellfish, smoked fish, deli products, sauces and frozen seafood. It was established by Dan Stern in 2009 and has been well supported by local people ever since. The Fish Shop is a chef's back up for a number of prestigious local restaurants such as Bianchi's and Little French.

"We try to buy as local as possible," says Dan. "After nearly a decade in the fish trade we have established contacts in Brixham, Looe, Plymouth and Newlyn fish markets, helping us to source the best in local fish. We are really lucky to be so close to the coast. Our suppliers literally stop and pick up oysters, mussels and crab meat for us on their drive up. We also buy from Fleetwood in Lancashire, Peterhead in Scotland and as far as Shetland."

The 'Var' salmon sold at The Fish Shop comes from the cold waters of the Faroe Islands. It is farmed in a low density free-range manner and guaranteed antibiotic- and chemical-free. The most local fish on the slab are line-caught from the Chew Valley.

The Fish Shop team are constantly on the lookout for new products too. The most recent example of this is an ancient breed of trout being farmed in Dorset which has twice the Omega 3 of a normal UK farmed trout. The Fish Shop offers selected products for nationwide delivery as well as a more local service in Bristol and Bath via Good Sixty, an eco-friendly bicycle-based food distribution company.

The Fish Shop also offers filleting courses in the evenings. Popular as presents, the two hour course covers all the basics of selecting and filleting fish such as mackerel, sea bass and plaice. Participants also learn to shuck and oyster and clean squid.

From suppliers to customers, Dan is all about good honest service and his favourite thing about working in a shop is the connection he makes with people. "In the Bristol shop we've even seen a first date (where the guy used our fish as the meal's star turn) lead to marriage and now they have a child together. Who knows...but what if he hadn't cooked her a fish supper that day? It's things that like that make this job so worthwhile."

The Fish Shop

Your Guide to Buying & Filleting Fresh Fish

When buying fish, always ask your fishmonger what's good and fresh. If they are any good, they will be delighted to talk you through what's in season, where it's from and when it was landed. These extra tips should allow you to buy and then fillet fresh fish with confidence.

Buying

Fish eyes can be deceptive; the fact that fish is packed and stored in ice means eyes can easily become dull after 24 hours. It's better to look at the gills, as bright red gills are always good sign. Brown and decaying gills are not. Next, stick your nose in it: fresh fish smells of the sea. Once you've rinsed your hands there should be no discernible fishy taint left. Slimy and stiff is a good thing; if the fish has a slimy bright sheen to it and is still stiff that's a great sign of freshness. Try to avoid fish with guts hanging out, and if the rib cage is lifting away from the fish when it has been gutted that is another bad sign.

When buying shellfish, always ask to see the tags for mussels and oysters so you know how long they have been out of the water. Both can easily last a week or a bit more if looked after properly. You can tell if a mussel is alive by tapping it hard on a board and seeing if it makes any attempt to close.

Cleaning Mackerel

Lay the fish on its back horizontally in front of you, with the head pointing left for right handers. Run your index finger under the gills and back towards you. Cut in close around the gills, then pinch low and hard to pull out the gills, and discard them.

Now place the fish on the board with the tail furthest away from you. Insert the knife through its anal vent and cut up the length of its belly towards the head. Pull out the guts and discard them. Give the mackerel a quick rinse in cold water and congratulations, you have a gutted fish.

Filleting Mackerel

Lay the fish out horizontally again with its gutted belly facing away from you. Lift up the fin just behind its head and cut just behind it at a 45° angle back towards the head, stopping when you reach the back bone. Make a turn and with your knife angled 5% down move along the fish towards the tail with broad strokes until you have released the fillet. Repeat for the other side. Debone both fillets by cutting down just behind the rib cage and scooping or dragging the few larger bones away. You should now have two lovely mackerel fillets. Well done!

For more video tips on fish filleting visit **www.lovethefishshop.com/videos**

FYNE FISH

What A Catch

A tempting combination of modern fishmonger, diverse seafood deli and innovative sushi maker, Fyne Fish is a business on a mission to bring quality fresh marine produce to Cumbria.

FYNE FISH
4d Station Street
Cockermouth
Cumbria
CA13 9QW

Telephone:
01900 827814
& Fyne Fish
@ Cranstons,
Penrith
01768 865736

Website:
www.fynefish.
net

Award-winning independent fishmongers featuring a large 'ready to eat' seafood deli selection, specialising in bespoke seafood platters and freshly made sushi.

Fyne Fish opened its doors in November 2011 in Cockermouth, the quaint town famed for being the birthplace of William Wordsworth. The fishmongers is owned and operated by husband and wife team John and Sharon Heron. The couple were inspired to start their venture by the lack of quality fresh fish available in the area, and have since made waves as winners of the National Fishmonger of the Year award at the Farmshop & Deli Awards in both 2018 and 2019.

It's a fishmongers with a difference, following traditional values yet employing a modern approach to provide the locals and visitors with a vast array of fresh fish and seafood, sourced where possible from the Cumbrian coast, as well as national and international waters. The wet fish counter ranges from traditional cod, salmon, haddock, plaice, sardines, kippers and scallops to the more adventurous squid, swordfish, monkfish, turbot and North Sea red bream. You'll also find shellfish from Shetland mussels to Dorset clams as well as West Cumbrian crab and lobster to North East Lindisfarne oysters. The seafood deli offers a stunning selection of ready-to-eat seafood, including Solway brown shrimps, Whitby crab, crayfish, roll mops, locally smoked salmon, Arbroath Smokies and fresh seaweed as well as their own shop-made pâtés, fish pies, cullen skink soup , dressed lobsters and bespoke seafood platters to meet any taste or budget.

In 2018, Fyne Fish joined the team at Cranstons Butchers, running a full fresh fish counter and deli at Cranstons Food Hall in Penrith while also supplying a selection of fish and deli products off the shelves in Cranstons' Orton Grange store. Around the same time, they moved premises in their hometown to a larger space on Station Street, their third shop in Cockermouth since starting out. Each store is slightly bigger than the last to reflect their growing customer base. Despite being a flourishing company, John, Sharon and their staff continue to be guided by the original passion, values and vision they had when starting out 11 years ago. The team are always full of recipe suggestions and new ideas for customers to try.

Fyne Fish have produced some of the most mouth-watering fusion-style sushi and sashimi, bringing a taste of the Orient to their customers, always fresh and exciting. They have decided to innovate once more, building a new space at the back of their Cockermouth shop which will soon host their relaunched sushi offering. Expect the same standard of hand-rolled freshly prepared sushi and sashimi and the return of their popular sushi schools. The room will also be used to celebrate fresh fish in a more general sense, promoting their wonderful selection of seafood and sharing knowledge through classes, talks, tasting evenings and more.

The combination of the day's freshly delivered catch and such friendly, efficient service draws customers from miles around. Simply put, the clue's in the name; fine fish is what these people are all about!

Fyne Fish An Indulgent Fish Pie

A fish pie can be as indulgent as you wish; use either a mixture of white fish (cod, haddock, pollock or hake) with added smoked fish or prawns, or go the whole hog and use luxury cuts of halibut, monkfish or tuna!

PREPARATION TIME: 20 MINUTES | COOKING TIME: 1 HOUR 15 MINUTES | SERVES 4

METHOD

Preheat the oven to 180°c. Peel the potatoes and cut them into small, even pieces, then boil in salted water until tender. Drain the potatoes and add a tablespoon of olive oil, 50ml of the fresh cream, and 15g of the butter. Mash until soft and creamy.

Cut the fish into evenly sized chunks and set aside. Thinly slice the leek and grate the carrot. Melt the remaining butter and olive oil in a pan, add the vegetables and fry for approximately 5 minutes, without allowing them to colour. Once the leek and carrot are soft, add the remaining cream. Bring to the boil, add the mustard and season to taste. Stir to combine, then reduce the heat and stir in the spinach, which will wilt immediately. Add the fish, chopped parsley and lemon juice, then taste to double check the seasoning.

Transfer the fish mix to an ovenproof dish, and carefully top with the creamy mashed potato. Place the fish pie on an oven tray (in case it bubbles over) and place the tray on the middle shelf of the preheated oven for 10-15 minutes. Brown under the grill if needed. If you have made the pie ahead of time and are cooking it from cold, the cooking time should be increased to 30-40 minutes.

Decorate the cooked pie with parsley stems, and serve with freshly cooked broccoli, asparagus or green beans on the side.

INGREDIENTS

1.5kg potatoes
2 tbsp olive oil
300ml fresh cream
40g butter
750g mixed fish fillets, skinned and boned (the choice of fish is yours entirely)
1 medium leek
1 carrot
1 tsp wholegrain mustard
2 handfuls of fresh spinach
1 bunch of fresh parsley, chopped
½ lemon, juiced
Salt and pepper
Broccoli, asparagus or green beans, to serve

"It's a fishmongers with a difference, following traditional values yet employing a modern approach."

Fyne Fish

GALTON BLACKISTON

Norfolk Hero

Proud holder of a Michelin star since 1998, Galton Blackiston is the Norfolk food scene's most famous son. He recently celebrated 30 years at Morston Hall while his latest venture, No.1 Cromer has proved a resounding success. Here, he shares his thoughts on what makes his home county so special.

"Well, how do I begin to sum up in a few words what Norfolk means to me? I was born and brought up here many moons ago, back in the days when holidays were rarely taken abroad, but instead by the British seaside; hence my deep affection for our wonderful Norfolk coastline.

MORSTON HALL HOTEL
The Street
Holt
Norfolk
NR25 7AA

Telephone: 01263 741041

Website: www. morstonhall.com

Morston Hall is an intimate country house hotel with a Michelin-starred restaurant.

Like many of us Norfolk folk, the lure of returning home having spent time away learning my trade was very strong. Once that dream was realised 25 years ago, my wife Tracy and I set about creating a little gem on the north Norfolk coast, Morston Hall. Our principles were simple back in those days, and they remain so now. We use very seasonal produce to create exciting yet achievable dishes. I'm biased I know, but in my eyes, there is no finer area to live and run a business or two.

Although the words seasonality and provenance might be trendy and hip at the moment, they have always played a huge part in the planning and success of Morston Hall. It makes sense to use vegetables and fruits when in season and 18 years of a Michelin star is surely testament to that. We have a wonderful plethora of seasonal produce in our back yard and it is a real pleasure being able to showcase just what this county has to offer; whether it be asparagus in May, samphire in July or Brussels sprouts in the winter. You name it; we've got it all in this wonderful county of ours.

The real beauty of Norfolk is the fact that as time passes, not a lot changes. We still have no motorway within the county and although life is very busy on the coast there remains a real sense of ruralness, which is something I have always treasured.

The striking dish overleaf is made with the freshest sea bass and squid, which is combined with salsify to make a delicious and simple risotto base.

We retained a Michelin star at Morston Hall for an unprecedented 18th successive year, as well as being awarded four AA rosettes. We're absolutely thrilled to have retained it, which means we've held the honour for every year since our first award back in 1999. We believe that's an unprecedented achievement for any restaurant in this part of the country."

Galton Blackiston
Pan Fried Wild Sea Bass with Squid Risotto and Nero Sauce

This striking dish is made with the freshest sea bass and squid, which is combined with salsify to make a delicious and simple risotto base.

PREPARATION TIME: 10 MINUTES | COOKING TIME: 20 MINUTES | SERVES 2

METHOD

Purée three of the cooked salsify sticks in a food processor or blender.

Cook the squid and add to the purée with some seasoning, then warm it through, adding a splash of lemon juice and the teaspoon of pickled sushi ginger.

Fry the remaining salsify in butter and season well.

Pan fry the sea bass in the rapeseed oil. Serve the sea bass on the squid risotto and place the pan fried salsify alongside. Serve with nero sauce.

INGREDIENTS

4 sticks of salsify, peeled and cooked
150g squid, roughly chopped
Splash of lemon juice
1 tsp pickled ginger
2 x 175g fillets of sea bass, de-scaled
2 tbsp rapeseed oil
Butter, for cooking
Salt and pepper
Nero sauce, to serve

Galton Blackiston
Cannelloni of Crab and Avocado with Elderflower Mayo

Galton Blackiston at Morston Hall has retained a Michelin star for an unprecedented 18th successive year. Here's one of their most popular dishes.

PREPARATION TIME: APPROX. 30 MINUTES | SERVES 6

METHOD

Carefully pick over the crab meat, making sure there is no shell in it. Place it into a bowl with the mayonnaise, chopped coriander, a good pinch of sea salt flakes and freshly ground black pepper. Spoon the mixture into a piping bag and place in the fridge until needed.

Peel and halve the avocados, remove the stone and then slice lengthways as thinly as possible.

Lay out six pieces of cling film on your work surface. Along the centre of each piece, lay the slices of half an avocado, about 20cm in length and slightly overlapping each slice. Sprinkle with lemon juice and lightly season with sea salt.

Pipe the crab meat just off centre along the length of the avocado slices. Then, using the cling film, roll up tightly like a sausage and tie each end. Place in the fridge to firm up.

Serve with elderflower mayonnaise and oven-roasted mini tomatoes.

INGREDIENTS

200g fresh white crab meat
1 tbsp mayonnaise
2 tbsp chopped coriander
3 ripe avocados
Lemon juice
Sea salt flakes and black pepper

To serve
Elderflower mayonnaise
Oven-baked mini tomatoes

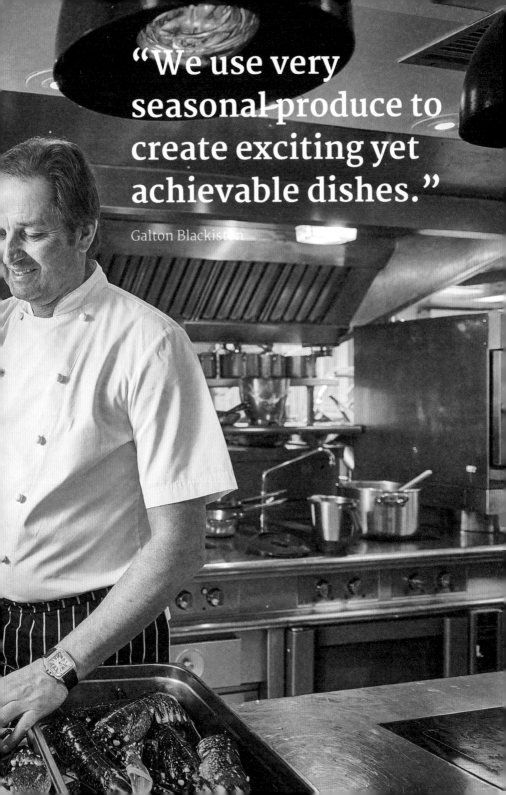

"We use very seasonal produce to create exciting yet achievable dishes."

Galton Blackiston

Charm, Period'

Family-run restaurant The Grove, Cromer joins all the dots to create an intimate, sumptuous experience...

THE GROVE, CROMER
The Grove
95 Overstrand
Road, Cromer
Norfolk
NR27 0DJ

Telephone: 01263
512412

Website: www.
thegrovecromer.
co.uk

Rosette-winning
family-run
restaurant whose
emphasis is on
inventive use of
local and seasonal
produce to
create succulent,
flavoursome
dishes.

You either have charm and character, or you don't. If you don't, well, they aren't things you can buy off the shelf. They're things that develop over time with the right approach. The Grove has both, but then it had something of a head start. Its origins date back to the mid-eighteenth century with the Barclays of banking fame making it their country retreat in the nineteenth century. The Graveling family have owned the property since the mid-twentieth century, but it's the approach that brothers Chris and Richard are taking in the twenty first that's really putting the place on the map.

Take the food. Those of us lucky enough to have been served vegetables fresh from the garden, or perhaps a fish caught only hours before, know it's a truism that the fresher the food, the greater the taste experience. This approach is a foundation stone of The Grove's menus. Where possible, what's presented on the plate comes from its gardens. Their output is supported by the very best Norfolk has to offer, which means diners experience some of the best produce Britain has to offer. Rare breed meat and poultry from local farms, award-winning cheeses from nearby dairies, and lobsters caught locally and to order in season by a long-established fishing family are just a few examples.

The emphasis is on simplicity, but that doesn't mean workaday. The Grove puts the very highest quality ingredients together in inventive, flavoursome ways, an approach that has won the establishment two AA rosettes. The Grove's delicious dishes are presented in equally exquisite period surroundings. The Green Room, which can be traced back to the original Georgian house, is available for private dining parties while The Study offers an elegant, refined experience. The food served in both springs from the same kitchen, overseen and supported by a formidable team to ensure that the quality and service remains outstanding in each.

In our health-conscious times where every calorie is counted, 'eat, drink, and be merry' has fallen far more out of favour than it should. The Grove believes the two aren't incompatible. Eat well, live well is an ethos at the heart of what it does. With charming cottages and yurts available for visitors and 'glampers' alike, there is no reason not to make a night of it, wake up refreshed the next morning, and perhaps go back for seconds. In 2021, in response to the pandemic, The Grove opened Sundown, which serves Norfolk tapas, pizzas and ice cream in a purpose-built giant tipi restaurant. Sundown has gone down a treat with locals and residents alike and is fast becoming one the coolest places to eat in Norfolk.

The Grove, Cromer
Pan Seared Skrei Cod with Pancetta, Razor Clam, Fennel & Pernod Chowder

This recipe was created by Reis Khalil, head chef at The Grove Cromer. For those that don't like clams, 200g of live mussels would also work well. Mussels should be closed before they are cooked, and if any remain open after a good shake, discard them.

PREPARATION TIME: 10-15 MINUTES | COOKING TIME: 30-35 MINUTES | SERVES 4

INGREDIENTS
1 tbsp vegetable oil
1 large onion, chopped
2 fennel bulbs, sliced
100g pancetta lardons
50ml Pernod
600ml fish stock
(bought or made)
225g new potatoes,
quartered
1 large leek, halved and
thinly sliced
4 Skrei Cod Supremes,
ideally about 4cm
thick
320g fish pie mix
(salmon, haddock and
smoked haddock)
400ml double cream
12-16 razor clams
Salt and pepper, to
taste
Small bunch of parsley,
chopped
Crusty bread, to serve

METHOD
Heat half the oil in a large saucepan over a medium heat, then add the onion, fennel and pancetta. Cook for 8-10 minutes until the onion is soft and the bacon is cooked, then add the Pernod. The alcohol will be cooked off during the process.

Preheat your oven to 180°c. Pour the fish stock into the pan and bring it up to a gentle simmer. Add the potatoes, cover, then simmer for 10-12 minutes until the potatoes are cooked through. Stir in the sliced leek.

Meanwhile, add the remaining oil to a frying pan (preferably cast iron) and get it smoking hot. Pat the cod dry with kitchen roll and season generously, then place skin side down in the pan. Sear the skin until it is golden brown and crispy, then flip the fish over and cook for a further 2 minutes before transferring to an ovenproof tray to finish cooking in the oven.

Tip the fish pie mix into the first pan and gently simmer for 4 minutes. Add the cream and razor clams, then simmer until the cream has reduced to your desired thickness and the clams have opened. Check the seasoning, adding salt as needed.

Remove the cod from the oven and check it's cooked by pressing the sides of the flesh to see if you can feel them flaking away from each other.

Put a large ladle of your chowder in a bowl and use a spatula to place the cod on top. Sprinkle with the parsley, then serve with some crusty bread and fresh cracked black pepper.

Clams not pictured.

"The fresher the food, the greater the taste experience."

The Grove, Cromer

Magnum Opus!

Fine dining, fine accommodation, and much, much more makes The Haughmond a must-visit venue.

THE HAUGHMOND
Pelham Road
Upton Magna
Shrewsbury
SY4 4TZ

Telephone: 01743 709198

Website: www.thehaughmond.co.uk

17th century modern coaching inn and 3 rosette restaurant located in the historic village of Upton Magna, an enviable position in the heart of Shropshire.

We all like word-of-mouth recommendations. After all, if those we know put us in the know, we feel we're in safe hands. But if that is backed up with award-winning critical acclaim, well, it's hard to go wrong. The Haughmond, a modern coaching inn in the picturesque village of Upton Magna, combines a glowing reputation among customers with a slew of awards, including 3 AA Rosettes, Michelin Guide and Good Hotel Guide listings, celebrating the culinary excellence and outstanding accommodation it offers.

Situated only a few miles from the medieval market town of Shrewsbury and the World Heritage site of Ironbridge, husband and wife owners Mel and Martin Board took on the project in 2012 with a clear vision for what they wanted to accomplish. Following a careful and considered restoration, The Haughmond has regained its place as not only the heart of Upton Magna and a true source of pride for the local community, but also a destination to visit and stay for travellers who come from near and far.

The Haughmond specialises in serving the best locally sourced produce in inventive menu combinations and providing great service in a welcoming environment. Those looking for something special will find much to enjoy in the 'Basil's Tastes of The Haughmond' menu, an exquisite 6-course celebration of the best seasonal ingredients Shropshire has to offer.

Following the same ethos, the lunch and dinner à la carte menus take a creative approach, maintaining value and overdelivering on expectation. The menus regularly change to accommodate the best seasonal ingredients at their peak, so repeat visits are very much the order of the day! A real jewel in Shropshire's foodie crown, The Haughmond is something special indeed.

All pictures except top right: Andy Hughes

The Haughmond
Pan Fried Mackerel, Broccoli, Almond & Lime

This is one of my all-time favourite flavour combinations. The broccoli and almond bring a perfectly bittersweet balance to the dish with the acidity of the lime cutting through the oily mackerel.

PREPARATION TIME: 30 MINUTES | COOKING TIME: 30 MINUTES | SERVES 4

METHOD

For the mackerel fillet
To start, make sure the mackerel fillets are pin boned. Mix 20g of the sea salt with 20g of the caster sugar and coat both sides of the mackerel with the cure. Leave to marinate for 20 minutes. Wash off under cold water and pat dry with kitchen roll.

For the almond dressing
Toast the flaked almonds in the oven at 150°c for 8 minutes or until golden brown. Leave to cool on the side. Whisk the remaining caster sugar, lime juice, lime zest, rapeseed oil, almond oil and 2g of sea salt together. Fold the cooled flaked almonds, diced apple and 10g of chopped chervil into the dressing.

For the broccoli purée
In a medium saucepan, bring the butter, water and 5g of sea salt to a simmer. Finely slice the broccoli including the stalk, then add to the pan along with the remaining chopped chervil. Bring back to a simmer and cook for 8 minutes, stirring occasionally. Strain off the broccoli, reserving the liquid. Blend the broccoli in a food processor until a thick smooth purée is formed, adding some of the liquid if the mixture is too thick.

For the tenderstem broccoli
Coat a frying pan with vegetable oil and bring to a medium heat, then add your tenderstem broccoli. Heat to a deep golden brown (approximately 2 minutes), then turn over and repeat the same process on the other side. Season with sea salt.

Cooking the mackerel
Coat a cold frying pan with vegetable oil and place the mackerel fillets in skin side down. Slowly bring the pan up to a medium heat (this will help to stop the skin from contracting and curling). Once the skin is golden brown, turn over for just 5 seconds and remove from the pan.

To serve
Mix the almond dressing and place in the middle of your plate, using the back of the spoon to spread it evenly around. Criss-cross the tenderstem broccoli, creating a platform for the mackerel. Place the mackerel on top and then dot the broccoli purée around the plate. Place the borage leaves in the purée to garnish.

INGREDIENTS
4 large mackerel fillets
30g sea salt
40g caster sugar
100g flaked almonds
100g fresh lime juice
2 limes, zested
50g cold pressed rapeseed oil
50g almond oil
1 Granny Smith apple (cored, peeled and finely diced)
30g chopped chervil
200g salted butter
200g water
1 large head of broccoli
100g tenderstem broccoli
Vegetable oil
Borage leaves

From India With Love

For authentic Indian food made with fresh produce, Mandira's Kitchen is Surrey's one-stop shop for delicious ready meals, catering, supper clubs and more, inspired by one woman's journey from East to West...

MANDIRA'S KITCHEN
Silent Pool
Shere Road
Albury
Guildford
GU5 9BW

Telephone: 01483 940 789

Website: mandiraskitchen.com

Surrey's one-stop shop for delicious ready meals, catering, supper clubs and more, all made with love to authentic Indian recipes.

Mandira grew up on a tea plantation in Assam: an "idyllic childhood" during which she experienced Indian food in all its shades and hues. However, when she later moved to the UK with her husband after living in Calcutta for a time, Mandira discovered that, contrary to people's expectations, she couldn't really cook. Indian food in the UK is very different to the regional cuisines she was used to, so she had to learn quickly in order to reclaim those flavours because "the best food comes out of the family home."

When her work in management consultancy came to a sudden stop, Mandira made a decision to pursue her newfound skill and her love for home-style dishes that carried a personal history with them. A trip back to India in 2016 provided the perfect opportunity for culinary exploration, and shortly afterwards Mandira hosted her first supper club for family, friends and food lovers with local influence. It was a real success and the business, simply and aptly named Mandira's Kitchen, then went from strength to strength.

There is now a dedicated manufacturing kitchen and event space on site – right next to Silent Pool Gin, with whom Mandira has recently collaborated to create an Orange and Gin Chutney – to provide customers and stockists with freshly prepared food, blast-chilled to preserve all the goodness and then frozen to be sold in farm shops all over the county, or bought online and shipped by overnight courier to any UK address. The venture still hosts supper clubs as well as offering cookery classes, and caters for events as varied as weddings, formal dinners for hundreds of people, anniversary celebrations for couples and more.

The team make sure everything is made with love to produce food that defies typical expectations of Indian ready meals. Nothing is 'oily or greasy' and not all contain chillies, because each creation has a story and comes from indigenous regional dishes that aren't formulaic or Anglicised. This commitment to quality and real flavour has brought Mandira's Kitchen recognition and a well-established place within the community, including accolades for innovation in retail, Great Taste stars and Product of the Year in the 2019 Surrey Life awards. The business always has something new up its sleeve, and Mandira is keen to continue developing her ideas and passion for offering home-style food.

Mandira's Kitchen
Kolapata Maach (Fish in Banana Leaves)

No proper wedding in Calcutta is complete without these morsels of deliciousness. The fish is smothered in a mixture of coconut, coriander and mustard, wrapped in banana leaves and then steamed or baked.

PREPARATION TIME: 10 MINUTES, PLUS 1 HOUR MARINATING | COOKING TIME: 20 MINUTES | SERVES 6

METHOD

Cut the fish fillet into five thick 5cm by 7.5cm pieces. If you cannot find banana leaves for this recipe, then just use tinfoil.

For the marinade

Blend all the ingredients together into a paste. If you are using desiccated coconut, you may need to add a little water to the mixture. The marinade needs to be a thick paste and not runny at all. Taste it to make sure it has enough salt and if you need it hotter, add more green chillies.

Gently rub the marinade into the fish, then cover and set aside for 30 minutes or so.

To prepare the banana leaves, wipe them with a damp tissue and then one by one, carefully wave them over an open flame (ideally on a gas hob) so that they are gently scorched. This makes them easy to wrap without cracking. Now lay them flat on a table.

Lay a piece of fish in the centre of each banana leaf (or piece of tinfoil) with some extra marinade. Now gently fold the leaf over the fish, like you are wrapping a parcel, and secure each one with a toothpick. Lay the parcels on a greased baking tray.

Preheat your oven to 180°c and bake for 20 minutes until the banana leaves are brown. Serve the fish with steamed rice.

INGREDIENTS

Any firm white fish fillet, as fresh as you can manage to find

5 pieces of banana leaf (each about the size of an A4 sheet of paper)

For the marinade
4 tbsp freshly grated coconut (frozen or unsweetened desiccated coconut will work too)
½ a bunch of fresh coriander leaves
1 or 2 green chillies (depending on how hot you want it)
1 tsp English mustard powder
¼ tsp salt
2 tbsp oil
½ a lemon, juiced

"Each creation has a story and comes from indigenous regional dishes."

Mandira's Kitchen

Crustacean Appreciation

This pioneering project based in Padstow is all about marine conservation in action, with a visitor centre giving people the opportunity to learn more about UK lobster fisheries and why their conservation efforts are so important.

THE NATIONAL LOBSTER HATCHERY
South Quay
Padstow
Cornwall
PL28 8BL

Telephone: 01841 533877

Website:
www.
nationallobster
hatchery.co.uk

A pioneering marine conservation, research and education charity and visitor education centre based in Padstow.

The National Lobster Hatchery is a small yet mighty marine conservation charity that aims to help conserve native lobster populations and ultimately protect the long term future of the UK's fishing heritage and all it supports. As well as their education and research outputs, they have a unique and innovative lobster stock enhancement programme. This involves raising baby lobsters at the hatchery until they reach the point where they are better able to survive in the wild. This is when they are released into our native waters, with the help of local fishermen and dive schools.

"I feel incredibly privileged to be playing a role in such an important pioneering project at the National Lobster Hatchery. As someone who loves nothing more than being at sea, fishing, and dining on delicious native seafood, it makes me happy to know I am helping to 'put back' when it comes to our vital but fragile marine resources," says business development manager Clare Stanley.

A female lobster can carry in the region of 4,000 to 40,000 eggs but only one of these eggs is expected to survive in the wild. The NLH's conservation programme helps improve the survival rate dramatically by helping to protect juvenile lobsters during their earliest life stages when they are most vulnerable, especially to predators. Their mission is becoming increasingly important, not just in the UK, but as a model for fisheries and coastal community management worldwide. With more than 75% of global fish stocks either exploited, depleted or recovering, and demand for seafood at an all-time high, they are not only helping to conserve vulnerable lobster populations in the UK, but educating the public and future recruits to the industry on the importance of not just a more sustainable fishery but also being sustainable in their everyday lives and consumer choices.

The NLH has received numerous awards for their charitable achievements and innovation, most recently a Silver Award for Best Wildlife Friendly Business and Bronze for Resilience and Innovation at the Cornwall Tourism Awards 2022. As a global centre of expertise, their work is also recognised internationally and the fascinating and fun educational visitor centre in Padstow welcomes over 45,000 visitors each year. The NLH have now released well over a quarter of a million juvenile lobsters into UK coastal waters and are confident that this is making a positive impact on the sustainability of Cornwall's lobster fishery and the communities that it supports.

© Alex Hyde

© Alex Hyde

© Alex Hyde

National Lobster Hatchery

Asian Style Oven Baked Sea Bass

This recipe was created by my lovely neighbour Chrissie Taylor and I love it! It also works with other white fish and I'd always opt to use one that is considered sustainable at the time, such as pollock. – Clare Stanley

PREPARATION TIME: 45 MINUTES | COOKING TIME: 20-30 MINUTES | SERVES 2

INGREDIENTS

1 whole sea bass (from a sustainable source)
Sea salt
Black pepper
2 cloves of garlic, crushed
3cm fresh ginger, peeled and grated
2 fresh red chillies, diced
2 lemongrass stalks, cut diagonally into small pieces
2 tbsp light soy sauce
1 small tin of coconut cream
Handful of cherry tomatoes
3 spring onions, chopped
Handful of fresh coriander, to taste

METHOD

Ensure the fish is fully cleaned and gutted with the gills and any threads within removed. I like to keep the head on but you can remove the head if preferred. Slash the flesh on both sides of the fish, if it's not already done, and season it inside and out with sea salt and black pepper.

Mix the crushed garlic, grated ginger, diced chilli and lemongrass together, plus a pinch of sea salt and black pepper. Finally, add the light soy sauce to the mixture. Let the whole fish marinate in this mixture for at least 30 minutes.

Place the fish, including all the remaining marinade, in a piece of foil and add the coconut cream. Wrap the foil around the fish and crimp the edges to seal it at the top, forming a parcel. Make sure there is still some space around the fish.

Place the foil parcel in the oven and bake for 20-30 minutes at 170°c. Halfway through the cooking time, remove the foil parcel from the oven, open it up and add the handful of cherry tomatoes and the chopped spring onions, making sure to close it again before putting it back in the oven for the remaining cooking time. Once fully baked, leave to stand for 5 minutes before opening the foil parcel.

To serve

I like to serve this dish with a few coriander leaves scattered on top and rice on the side, fried lightly with a little butter and light soy sauce, along with some seasonal leafy veg.

See www.cornwallgoodseafoodguide.org.uk for advice on which fish are recommended as sustainable.

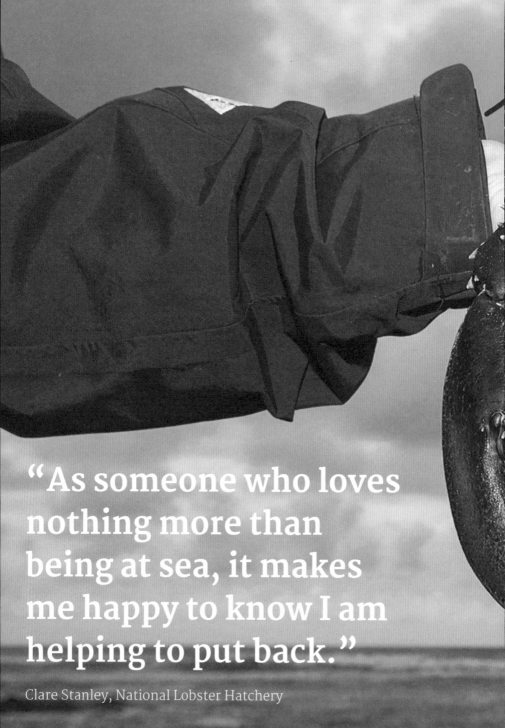

"As someone who loves nothing more than being at sea, it makes me happy to know I am helping to put back."

Clare Stanley, National Lobster Hatchery

© Alex Hyde

THE OYSTER CLUB

Join The Club

April 2019 saw the opening of a new seafood-focused restaurant by Adam and Natasha Stokes, located just a few hundred metres from their Michelin-starred restaurant Adam's in the heart of Birmingham.

With an Oyster Bar, a menu focusing on seafood and a stunning wine list, The Oyster Club offers a casual and relaxed approach to dining, while maintaining the high standards set by Adam and Natasha. The restaurant serves British seafood dishes such as Stokes' take on fish and chips, while fresh oysters are shucked in front of diners.

THE OYSTER CLUB
43 Temple St
Birmingham
B2 5DP

Telephone:
0121 643 6070

Website:
www.the-oyster-club.co.uk

Oysters, caviar and seafood entrées, plus Sunday roasts, presented in a refined restaurant with a bar.

The Oyster Club takes its name from a group of intellectuals and scientists who used to meet in Edinburgh in the 1770s to debate and exchange ideas over dinner. "It seemed the perfect name for this place," says Adam. "I wanted to encourage a neighbourhood feel; we offer a friendly relaxed service and have regular diners who do see The Oyster Club as a club where they can meet and catch up with each other over a plate of oysters."

The Oyster Club won a Michelin Plate in its first year of opening, an achievement which head chef Rosie Moseley rates as one of her career highlights to date. "At The Oyster Club we always aim for the highest standard with every service - that takes so much teamwork and focus. I speak to our suppliers every day about the best ingredients available and what we can get in. We are a seafood-focused restaurant with a lot of grill dishes, so freshness is everything to us."

The Oyster Club's fresh seafood offering in Birmingham is unique for the city centre and has helped distinguish its experience from the host of culinary options across the city.

Rosie explains that "it's a really unique selling point for a location such as ours, but we also make sure that diners can enjoy our other non-seafood dishes, comfortable in the knowledge that the quality is still as high as it can possibly be. I feel that cooking has moved away from the more unusual cooking methods and techniques we've seen in years gone by and today's methods are built around simplicity. At The Oyster Club we have a very traditional and classic approach to cookery: everything is in the pan and it's all about the produce."

The Oyster Club
Dressed Crab with Crispy Chicken Skin and Avocado

This fantastic dish is something we think highlights the quality of the produce in a way that is more traditional and simple but still delicious. Our classic approach to cooking is all about the flavour without the overly complicated techniques.

INGREDIENTS

1 live brown crab
(around 1kg)
Salt
1 Granny Smith apple
2 tbsp tomato ketchup
20g chives, finely chopped
3 limes, juiced
1 pink grapefruit, segmented
4 slices of sourdough toast or croutons

For the mayonnaise
2 large egg yolks
1 tsp Dijon mustard
2 tsp chardonnay vinegar
300ml vegetable oil

For the avocado purée
2 avocados
40g lime juice
60ml water
9g red chilli
35g shallot, chopped
100ml olive oil

For the chicken skin
50g chicken skin

PREPARATION TIME: 1 HOUR 15 MINUTES | COOKING TIME: 35 MINUTES | SERVES 4

METHOD

For the crab

Place the crab in the freezer half an hour before cooking. Bring a large pan of water to the boil and season with salt. Once boiling, drop in the crab and cook for 12 minutes, then fully submerge in iced water to halt the cooking process. When cool enough to handle, remove all the legs and claws from the crab by twisting them away from the body. Holding the head, use your thumbs to push the body up and out of the hard top shell. Remove and discard the dead man's fingers, stomach sack and any hard membranes. Using a spoon, scoop out any brown meat from the top shell and save for another recipe). Using a crab pick or the handle of a spoon, scoop out any meat you can find in the crevasses of the head and place in a bowl. With a heavy knife or mallet, break open the crab claws. Pick out the white meat and place in the bowl. With the knuckles and legs, pick the meat out with the crab pick or, if needed, tap them open with your knife.

For the mayonnaise

Place the egg yolks, mustard and vinegar in a container. Using a whisk or a hand blender, slowly add the oil until emulsified, then season with salt.

Peel and grate the Granny Smith apple. Remove any excess juice by placing the apple in muslin cloth and squeezing it. Mix the white crab meat with three tablespoons of your mayonnaise and the ketchup. Add the grated apple, chopped chives, a pinch of salt and the lime juice to the crab. Mix together and season to taste.

For the avocado purée

Place all ingredients except the oil in a blender and blend until smooth. Slowly add the oil and a pinch of salt. Place in a piping bag or plastic bottle, ready to serve. Preheat the oven to 180°c. Scrape the excess fat off the chicken skin with a sharp knife. Cover a baking tray with parchment and thinly spread the chicken skin on top. Season with salt. Place another piece of parchment over the top and then another flat tray so the chicken skin is sandwiched between the two. Cook in the oven for 20 minutes until golden and crispy.

To finish

Place a ring mould on a plate, spoon in the crab mix and compress the meat. Remove the ring mould and add a few dots of avocado purée, five grapefruit segments and a few shards of crispy chicken skin. Serve on sourdough toast or with croutons.

PRITHVI

A Fine Spice

When it comes to serving Indian food to the Great British public, Prithvi in Cheltenham is breaking the mould. Expertly combining the experience of fine dining with Bangladeshi spices and flavours, it's no wonder they've achieved accolades alongside some of the country's best Michelin-starred establishments.

PRITHVI
37 Bath Road
Cheltenham
GL53 7HG

Telephone: 01242 226229

Website: www. prithvirestaurant.com

A refined and sophisticated approach to Indian dining in intimate and relaxed surroundings.

Working in an Indian restaurant from the age of thirteen (incidentally on the premises where Prithvi now stands), owner Jay Rahman has since experienced the industry full circle. From the heat of the kitchen to front of house service at luxury hotels and top restaurants, his experience enabled him to achieve the perfect balance when it came to opening his own place back in 2012.

"I wanted to challenge what Indian food was about in the UK. Nothing has really changed since the 1960s, and there's so much more to it than a huge plateful of curry."

Prithvi's menu delicately combines Indian spices and methods with premium British produce, and each dish is served with as much refinement as any fine dining French or British restaurant.

Their suppliers are carefully selected for their quality, locality and sustainability, with menus adapting to reflect the seasons. It's unlikely you'll find scallops, venison, halibut or duck at your average curry house but they often appear at Prithvi, and it's not just the food that receives exceptional attention; customers are looked after far beyond the last bite.

"The experience doesn't end when the customer leaves," says Jay. "Whether they come in the next week or six months down the line, it's a continuous experience. I respond to all emails and feedback personally and with the same care and consideration as I would to someone dining."

These little touches haven't gone unnoticed either, with Prithvi featured among top industry names for numerous awards. They came in sixth out of 100 in the Travellers' Choice Fine Dining Restaurant Awards, amongst the likes of The Fat Duck, L'Enclume and Adam's. In 2016 they were also number six in the list of top ten restaurants in the country on Trip Advisor.

"To be associated with such highly regarded restaurants is a great honour. Indian food is often looked at as a lower calibre to other cuisines, but we're really proud to be recognised amongst prestigious and acclaimed restaurants. To be with, and even above, restaurants with Michelin stars is humbling."

Prithvi Halibut with Black Mustard Jus

A staple in the north eastern region of Bangladesh, the jus is fantastic with all seafood. Halibut is a meaty and fragrant fish tht lends itself to th strong and earthy roasted mustard. This dish is best accompanied by a root vegetable.

PREPARATION TIME: 15 MINUTES | COOKING TIME: 30 MINUTES | SERVES 4

INGREDIENTS

For the mustard jus
¼ tbsp black mustard seeds
4 tbsp rapeseed oil
6 cloves of garlic, chopped
1½ medium onions, sliced
Table salt
3 bay leaves
½-1 tsp ground turmeric
½-1 tsp ground coriander
½-1 tsp curry powder
½-1 tsp chilli powder
Fresh coriander, chopped

For the halibut
1 tsp rapeseed oil
½ tsp ground turmeric
½ tsp ground coriander
½ tsp curry powder
½ tsp chilli powder
4 halibut fillets, boned and skinned
Sea salt

For the broccoli
240g tenderstem broccoli
Butter
Black pepper, crushed
¼ tsp curry powder

METHOD

Prepare the black mustard jus beforehand. Lightly toast the black mustard seeds in a dry skillet, then crush using a pestle and mortar. In a deep pan, heat the rapeseed oil on a low heat. When warm (it will not work if the oil is too hot) add the garlic and let it lightly brown. Add the onions and stir. Add salt to taste, starting with quarter of a tablespoon, and stir, making sure it doesn't catch the bottom of the pan. Drop in the bay leaves.

Once the onions have lost most of their liquid, start adding hot water, half a cup at a time. Once the water has reduced add another half a cup. Do this four times or until the onions and garlic have become soft. Now add the spices: use half a teaspoon if you like it mild or a whole teaspoon if you prefer it spicier. Stir often and don't let them catch the bottom of the pan. Keep adding a small amount of hot water to stop the spices from burning. The spices will take on a vibrant colour.

Add the crushed black mustard seeds to the pan and stir in for 5-6 minutes. Add 1½ cups of hot water, raise the heat to medium, cover and let it simmer for 10 minutes. Lastly, stir in the freshly chopped coriander to taste.

For the halibut
In a flat dish, combine the rapeseed oil, turmeric, coriander, curry powder, chilli powder, and sea salt using a teaspoon. Add the halibut and softly massage the fish all over with the marinade. You can fry the fish as soon as you're ready; there's no need to leave it to marinate for this dish. Shallow fry the halibut with a little more rapeseed oil on a medium to low heat. For a crunchy crust, cook for 3-4 minutes on each side, or 2-3 minutes if you prefer it softer.

For the broccoli
Boil the broccoli in a pan of water for 2 minutes. Tip into a colander and run under the cold tap water or place in a bowl with ice and water to refresh. Heat a knob of butter in a skillet and add the broccoli. Season with sea salt, crushed black pepper and, most importantly, a sprinkling of curry powder. Stir fry for 3-4 minutes on a medium heat.

To serve
On a deep plate, pour the mustard jus into the centre and place the halibut on top with the tenderstem broccoli on the side.

"I wanted to challenge what Indian food was about in the UK."

Jay Rahman, Prithvi

Yas Queen!

A modern dining pub in South Milford, The Queen o' t' owd Thatch has built up a reputation as one of the best places to eat in West Yorkshire, with its seafood dishes in particular creating waves.

THE QUEEN O' T' OWD THATCH
101 High Street
South Milford
LS25 5AQ

Telephone: 01977 685096

Website: www. theqott.com

Yorkshire pup for drinkers, diners and dogs. We use Yorkshire produce for our seasonal menus, serve a fabulous Sunday lunch and excellent wines, cocktails and well-kept cask ales.

An affinity for pubs runs in the blood for Kirsty, who has been running The Queen o' t' owd Thatch with her partner Annie since 2013. Her grandfather had run a pub and her father was a master brewer, so she grew up in and around the industry. She got her first job as a pot wash aged 15 and from there she worked in every type of venue imaginable – from small local inns to fine dining establishments – all over the country. When she met Annie, a passionate foodie, gardener and natural people-person, they discovered a joint ambition of running their own pub. Annie left her successful career in the charitable sector and they gravitated back to Kirsty's Yorkshire roots to run The Queen o' t' owd Thatch in South Milford.

The place became a symbol of everything they loved in a pub: cosy and friendly, with quality food and drink for guests to enjoy, plus a stylish beer garden to boot. The Queen o' t' owd Thatch is an enthusiastically dog friendly venue too. The drinks are as important as the food, and they serve only those beers, wines and cocktails they enjoy themselves. Like everything else, if Annie and Kirsty don't believe in it, it doesn't make the cut. However, it's the food that has really helped this pub make a name for itself, winning the Observer Food Monthly Award for best Sunday dinner in 2018 and being listed as a runner up in every other year since opening.

Part of that success is down to Kirsty's passion for great local produce and the ingredients used generally come from within 20 miles, some of it from Annie's own kitchen garden. It's in the fish and seafood dishes on the menu that Kirsty's craft really shines through, allowing her to utilise traditional techniques such as curing to enhance the flavours of the high quality ingredients. To best showcase her fantastic creations, they frequently run popular food and wine pairing events, using their knowledge of serving (and drinking) great wine to perfectly marry with Kirsty's exquisite food. These luxurious evenings always revolve around a theme and are occasionally focused on seafood, and Annie says that these have been some of their favourite nights in the pub.

Kirsty says that "seafood has been a big part of my life and growing up I used to go to the coast with my grandad to find crabs. Much of my love of food comes from spending time with my grandad and I have fond memories of going to the East Coast, collecting a crab, taking it home, boiling it whole and sitting in the kitchen picking away at it. I'm also really passionate about fish and chips – I genuinely love it! We like to use a lot of ingredients from Yorkshire, but I often take my inspiration for the dishes from France, Spain and Japan because seafood is really central to their cooking. I feel like it's a shame that we don't make more of it in this country, given that we are an island. You need to treat fish delicately and with care, which makes it really satisfying to work with."

The Queen o' t' owd Thatch Cured and Scorched Sardine on Sourdough Toast

They may seem like a humble ingredient but sardines are packed with flavour, and this punchy ketchup complements them superbly. We love these on sourdough but you can of course use your favourite type of toasted bread.

PREPARATION TIME: 3 HOURS | COOKING TIME: 10 MINUTES | SERVES 4

METHOD

For the sardines

Ask your fishmonger to butterfly the sardines for you or if they won't, there are videos on YouTube. You want a nice, fat one, ideally Cornish.

Warm the mirin, rice wine vinegar and sea salt through gently but do not let the mixture boil. When the salt has dissolved, leave to cool.

Once cooled, put the curing liquid in a non-metal container and submerge the sardines. Lay baking parchment over the top of the liquid to make sure they stay fully submerged.

After 2 hours and 30 minutes, rinse under a cold tap and pat dry.

For the ketchup

This will make more than you need but will keep for up to a week in the fridge. While the sardines are curing, chop the tomatoes, peppers and shallot roughly, toss with the garlic cloves and salt, then spread out in a roasting tin and drizzle with the olive oil. Roast at 200°c for 40 minutes, stirring every 10 minutes. After 40 minutes, add the bay leaf, rosemary, ground pepper, paprika and cumin. Mix thoroughly and roast for another 15 minutes. Blend the mixture and then pass the ketchup through a fine sieve.

To serve

Slice a nice piece of sourdough per person, rub each slice with extra virgin olive oil and a cut garlic clove and toast until golden.

Turn the grill to its highest heat and grill the cured sardines (or use a blow torch, if you prefer) on the skin side just until they start to blister.

Place the sardines atop the sourdough, dot with the delicious ketchup and drizzle with your best olive oil... That's it!

INGREDIENTS

For the sardines
4 butterflied sardines
75g mirin
35g rice wine vinegar
10g sea salt

For the ketchup
4 plum vine tomatoes
4 green peppers
1 shallot
3 cloves of garlic
1 tsp sea salt
25ml olive oil
1 bay leaf
Sprig of rosemary
½ tsp ground pepper
½ tsp paprika
¼ tsp ground cumin

To serve
Good sourdough or your favourite bread
Extra virgin olive oil

"I'm also really passionate about fish and chips – I genuinely love it!"

The Queen O't'owd Thatch

SCUTCHERS

Culinary Classics

Nick and Diane Barrett have created something special within the 16th century walls at Scutchers restaurant, and it has been drawing in hungry locals for over three delectable decades.

SCUTCHERS
Westgate Street
Long Melford
Sudbury
Suffolk
CO10 9DP

Telephone: 01787 310200

Website: www. scutchers.com

Fine dining restaurant open Thursday, Friday and Saturday for lunch and dinner. Scutchers also cater for occasions such as weddings, business events and large parties.

Accomplished cooking is the order of the day at Scutchers. With 44 years of experience behind him, Nick Barrett has been cooking since he left the classroom aged 16. The years of traditional training are evident in the ethos of the kitchen. This is proper cooking, and it's a joy to behold.

Nick and his wife Diane bought the attractive hall house, which dates back to 1530, over 30 years ago. With Nick heading up the kitchen, Diane expertly taking charge of front of house and a long-standing set of loyal staff, this dedicated team have been rewarded with success after success... their collection includes Good Food Guide awards and a Michelin Bib Gourmand.

However, this husband and wife duo don't have time to sit back and admire their accolades. When they are not running the restaurant, they are busy smoking their own salmon on the premises, which they supply all over the country and feature on the restaurant menu of course.

It's this commitment to raw ingredients that sets this family-run business apart. The philosophy here is simple: proper food, cooked well. They're open for service on Thursdays, Fridays and Saturdays to the public, while the venue is also available for private bookings throughout the week.

Fish and cuts of meat are all delivered whole to the restaurant, where they are filleted or butchered on site. Only by understanding the basics can chefs really do ingredients justice, and, as they source the finest possible ingredients from around the UK, doing them justice is a priority here.

Loyal customers return time and time again to enjoy the classic favourites and seasonal specials. "Lots of our customers have become friends over the years," says Nick, who is on first-name terms with many of the regulars.

With such a warm welcome by Diane, a relaxed atmosphere and exemplary award-winning cooking, this established gem is the epitome of fine dining without the fuss.

Scutchers

Fillet of Wild Turbot with Asparagus, Broad Beans and Bacon

One of the most popular fish dishes on our menu, turbot never fails to impress. Served up with salty bacon, fresh asparagus, broad beans and a light and refreshing dressing, this irresistible recipe is a celebration of colour and flavour on the plate.

PREPARATION TIME: 20-25 MINUTES | COOKING TIME: 15 MINUTES | SERVES 4

METHOD

Blanch the tomatoes in boiling water for 20 seconds, then plunge them into cold water. Remove the skins, which should now come away easily, and cut the tomatoes into quarters. Remove and discard the seeds and cut the flesh into small dice. Set aside.

Cook the asparagus in a pan of salted boiling water for 3-4 minutes, then refresh in cold water. Drain and set aside.

INGREDIENTS

2 large tomatoes
1 bunch of asparagus, woody ends snapped off
4 x 180g turbot fillets, skinned, plus 8 small fingers of turbot
Plain flour, for coating
1 egg, beaten
Panko breadcrumbs, for coating
2 tbsp lemon juice
8 tbsp olive oil
Pinch of sugar
100g broad beans, blanched and skins removed
4 rashers of unsmoked streaky bacon, cooked and cut into strips (optional)
A few chives, snipped
Oil, for deep-frying
Salt and black pepper

Preheat the grill to high. Place the turbot fillets on a buttered baking tray and season with salt and pepper. Grill the turbot for 5-7 minutes until cooked through (depending on the thickness of the fish).

Place a little flour in one bowl, the beaten egg in a second and the breadcrumbs in a third. Dip the fingers of turbot first in the flour, then the egg and finally the breadcrumbs. Heat the oil in a heavy-bottomed pan or deep fat fryer. Deep fry the turbot fingers in the hot oil until golden and cooked through. Drain on kitchen roll.

Mix the lemon juice, olive oil and sugar together and season with salt and pepper to make a dressing. When the turbot is cooked, warm the dressing in a pan with the asparagus, broad beans, bacon strips, diced tomato and chives.

Spoon the dressed accompaniment onto serving plates, place the turbot fillets on top and then add 2 deep-fried turbot fingers on top of each portion.

"Only by understanding the basics can chefs really do ingredients justice."

Nick Barrett, Scutchers

Sussex Food Heroes

Village fishmongers Veasey & Sons have scooped some impressive awards in their first ten years of business, and it's not surprising considering the talent, passion and knowledge they have also accumulated over this time.

Back in 2009, life was very different for owners Chris and Dan. Dan was working as a chef, while Chris was a fisherman. Chris was looking into ways he could sell his catch directly to customers. He began at East Grinstead farmers' market, and, following success there, he joined forces with chef Dan to open their own fishmongers in Forest Row.

VEASEY & SONS
17 Hartfield Road
Forest Row
East Sussex
RH18 5DN

Telephone: 01342 822906

Website: www. veaseyandsons. co.uk

Fish the way it should be, fished the way it should be.

Despite not being by the coast, this village fishmongers has certainly made waves and it's hard to believe that Veasey & Sons has only been in business since 2010, considering the list of accolades they have gathered so far. Awarded The Best Food Shop in Sussex twice, a Sussex Life award for "Outstanding Customer Service" and twice National Fishmonger of the Year, they were also finalists of BBC Radio 4's Food & Farming Awards (for Best Local Food Retailer) and Sussex Life Awards (for High Street Hero).

Chris's fishing boat is still a special part of the business. What they don't fish themselves, they source from reputable suppliers with a focus on wild British fish. Depending on the time of year, the counter can contain huss, whiting, hake, line-caught sea bass, mackerel, gurnard, and they even catch their own cod in season, something that is a world away from the supermarket offerings.

The whole team are passionate cooks and love to give cooking tips. Being part of the process every step of the way (fishing, landing, weighing and grading, storage, preparation, smoking and cooking) means there is nothing they do not know about their products.

As well as fresh fish, they specialise in smoked fish, which they prepare in-house. Home-smoked cod, salmon and haddock is then used in their handmade pâtés too. They also have an on-site production kitchen and offer a fantastic selection of prepared items. From fish pies and fishcakes to sauces and soups, they are a one-stop shop. For those not living near Forest Row, Veasey & Sons can be found at a number of markets in Sussex, Kent, Surrey and London; find the details of your nearest market on their website.

Top right photo: Archie Repchuk / www.archierepchuk.com / @archie.repchuk.photography

Veasey & Sons Classic Fishcake

An absolute shop favourite, easily made ahead of time and refrigerated for up to three days. You can even fry them off and run them through the oven to warm them up.

PREPARATION TIME: 15 MINUTES | COOKING TIME: 40 MINUTES | MAKES 6

INGREDIENTS

500g Veasey & Sons Mixed Fish Mix
350g Naturally Smoked Haddock, skinned, boned and diced
500ml milk
1 bay leaf
1 unwaxed lemon, zested and juiced
1kg Maris Piper potatoes, peeled and chopped
1 bunch of spring onions, sliced
1 tsp Dijon mustard
1 tbsp mayonnaise
50g capers, drained and roughly chopped
50g cornichons, drained and roughly chopped
1 tbsp finely chopped flat leaf parsley
1 tbsp finely chopped chives
Plain flour
3 eggs, beaten
Panko breadcrumbs
Sunflower oil
Salt and pepper

METHOD

Place all the fish into a deep frying pan, cover with the milk, add the bay leaf and half the lemon juice, then season with salt and pepper. Cook for 5 minutes until the fish is flaky, drain well and set aside.

Place the potatoes into a large saucepan, bring to the boil and simmer until tender, then drain and mash thoroughly, seasoning to taste. Mix the mashed potato with the spring onion, mustard, mayonnaise, capers, cornichons, flat leaf parsley, chives and lemon zest, then carefully fold the fish into the mix.

Prepare 3 deep dishes, the first with plain flour, the second with beaten egg and a little milk, and the third with the panko breadcrumbs.

Divide the mix into 6 equal portions, shape each one into a thick fishcake, then roll in the flour, the egg and then the breadcrumbs to coat.

Heat a large frying pan and add sunflower oil to a depth of 1cm, then place the fishcakes into the pan and slowly fry until golden brown and hot in the middle.

These are lovely served with a dressed green salad, a good tartare sauce and some juicy caperberries. Enjoy!

Veasey & Sons

Crispy Fried Sussex Gurnard Fillet with Curried Crab Sauce

A hugely flavoursome dish made using pot–caught Sussex crab and locally abundant gurnard. You can make the sauce first and set aside to keep warm while you finish the fish. Also, feel free to use a hotter curry powder if you like more spice.

PREPARATION TIME: 10 MINUTES | COOKING TIME: 15 MINUTES | SERVES 4

METHOD

For the sauce

Melt a knob of butter in a small frying pan, add the shallot and garlic and cook over a medium heat until softened. Add the curry powder and cinnamon stick, cook out for 1 minute, then add the wine. Reduce the mixture by half, then add the double cream. When the sauce returns to a simmer, add the dressed crab and bring back up to a light simmer, then remove the cinnamon stick and check the seasoning (the sauce should be well seasoned and punchy by this point). Blend the sauce in a food processor and set aside.

For the fish

In a large bowl, mix the plain flour, curry powder, salt and pepper. Add the gurnard fillets and mix through. Knock off the excess flour from the fillets and set aside. Heat a large thick-bottomed frying pan over a medium to high heat and add the butter and oil. Fry the gurnard fillets, starting skin side down, for 2 minutes per side. Lift the gurnard from the pan onto kitchen paper to drain off any excess oil.

To serve

This dish would be great served with steamed buttered vegetables. We recommend Chantenay carrots, asparagus and crushed Jersey Royal potatoes garnished with micro coriander. Layer the sauce, potatoes, vegetables and fish as per the photo.

INGREDIENTS

For the sauce

1 shallot, finely chopped
3 cloves of garlic, crushed
1 tsp mild curry powder
1 cinnamon stick
75ml white wine
100ml double cream
1 x 225g (8oz) dressed crab

For the fish

3 tbsp plain flour
1 tsp mild curry powder
Salt and pepper
4 medium gurnard, filleted and pin-boned
50g butter
1 tbsp vegetable oil

W STEVENSON & SONS

Catch of the Day

With one of the largest privately-owned fleets in Britain, the historic W Stevenson catch, land and sell the finest quality fresh fish from their fishmongers in Newlyn.

W STEVENSON & SONS
The Strand, 76 A Strand, Newlyn Penzance TR18 5HA

Telephone: 01736 330713

Website: wstevenson.co.uk

With over 100 years in the fishing industry and one of the largest privately-owned fleets in Britain, they catch, land and sell the finest quality fresh fish from Newlyn, Cornwall.

W Stevenson's story started over 100 years ago as a family fishing business perfectly situated in the town of Newlyn, just outside Penzance down in the far south west of Cornwall. The Cornish fishing industry is extremely diverse, and the coastal waters there are abundant with a rich variety of fish, meaning it is not unusual for the fish market to have 35 different species, all fresh, responsibly sourced and landed daily. Fishing has been a way of life in Newlyn for generations and W Stevenson are proud to be a part of that rich heritage. Today, their core fleet is still fishing out of the tidal port of Newlyn Harbour every day and their Cornish fishmongers is just a stone's throw from the Newlyn fish market and the harbour.

W Stevenson is also proud to have the first female Master Fishmonger, Elaine Lorys, running the fishmongers in Newlyn. "I've worked at Stevenson's for more than 25 years now and loved every minute of it! To do my job, you need a wide knowledge of everything to do with the fishing industry and sustainability, as well as filleting methods. I work in the shop, preparing the products and serving customers. From there, I can see our boats through the window and the fish market is about 100 feet away – it doesn't get much fresher than that!"

The boats Elaine casts an eye on through the shop window land everything from Cornish sole (megrim), plaice, monkfish and sardines to hake, dover, and lemon sole. They have one of the largest privately owned fleets in Britain, which allows them to control the entire process, from catch to customer, taking pride in providing the highest quality fish for your plate every time.

They also work closely with Cornish and national governing bodies to support new fishing methods, firmly believing that it is of paramount importance to their industry that they all work together to secure long term sustainable fishing practices. Victoria Townsend's words sum up the ethical ethos and goals of the business perfectly:

"We will continue fishing, providing employment for the next generation, and working with the Newlyn community to build an even stronger industry for the future. Our mission is simple: to ensure that the high quality, fresh Cornish fish landed by our boats is a staple on every family's weekly menu, now and in the future. We have such a wealth of high-quality British fish and we should all embrace what our waters can provide and eat more locally caught fish."

W Stevenson & Sons Fun Breaded Goujons with Slaw

Learning to pané – which means coating in flour, egg, then breadcrumbs so it's ready to cook – your own fish goujons is an excellent skill to master at home. You can cook fresh fish without any fuss and it's a real crowd-pleaser!

PREPARATION TIME: 5 MINUTES | COOKING TIME: 10 MINUTES | SERVES 2

METHOD

Learning to pané is very simple and a versatile way to reduce food waste by using leftover bread to make your own breadcrumbs. Adding herbs, sea salt and spices to the crumb mixture is a lovely way to season seafood and provides texture to the moist, flaky fish hidden beneath.

Prepare your hake by chopping it into scampi-sized medallions and dusting them with the seasoned flour. Preheat the oil to 180°c in a large deep pan or fryer.

Pané the hake by dipping each piece in the beaten egg and then coating in the panko breadcrumbs mixed with paprika.

Working in small batches, fry the hake goujons in the hot oil for 4-5 minutes until the breadcrumbs are golden brown and the fish is perfectly cooked. Place on a sheet of kitchen roll to drain off excess oil before serving.

For the slaw, simply combine all the ingredients, coating the veg in mayo. Season to taste and finish with a squeeze of lemon. Garnish with pickles and barbecue sauce for a Cajun style twist.

INGREDIENTS

400g hake
2 tbsp plain flour, seasoned
2 eggs, beaten
75g panko breadcrumbs
1 tsp smoked sweet paprika
Vegetable oil, for frying

For the slaw
1 spring onion, finely sliced
1 carrot, grated
¼ cabbage, shredded
1 tsp finely chopped chives
1 tbsp mayonnaise
1 tsp lemon juice
Pinch of salt

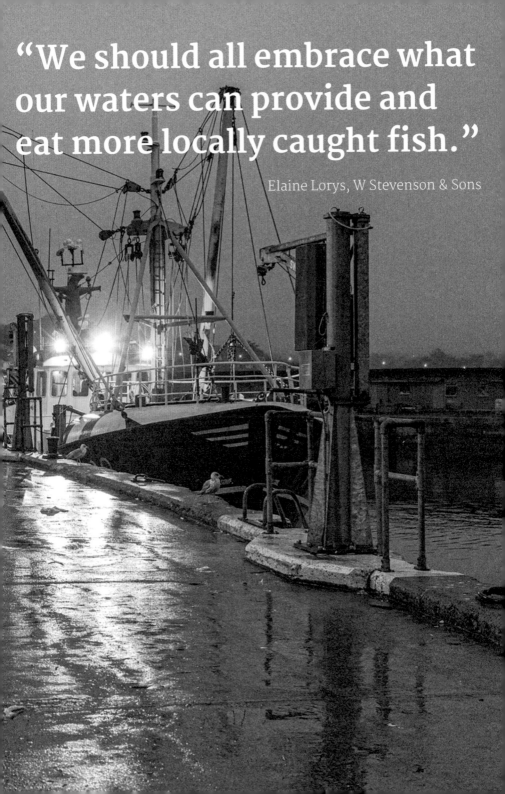

"We should all embrace what our waters can provide and eat more locally caught fish."

Elaine Lorys, W Stevenson & Sons

WELLS CRAB HOUSE

Quite A Catch

With a beautiful setting in one of Norfolk's picturesque fishing towns, Wells Crab House is the perfect place to enjoy the freshest seafood, straight from the boat to the plate.

WELLS CRAB HOUSE SEAFOOD RESTAURANT
38-40 Freeman Street, Wells-next-the-Sea Norfolk NR23 1BA

Telephone: 01328710456

Website: www.wellscrabhouse.co.uk

Wells Crab House offers a dining experience centred around beautifully prepared local and seasonal seafood dishes on the beautiful north Norfolk coast.

Wells-next-the-Sea enjoys an enviable location on the north Norfolk coast. A bustling seaside town during the summer, it is also a popular spot year-round thanks to the outstanding natural beauty of the landscape. At the heart of the town is the award-winning Wells Crab House, which reopened with its new name in 2016 following a refurbishment by owners Kelly and Scott.

The husband and wife team have many years of experience in the hospitality industry, and their passion for food and customer service has helped them to make Wells Crab House one of the area's most popular dining spots, with the Eat Norfolk Food and Drink Awards even bestowing them with the prestigious Restaurant of the Year and Outstanding Front of House Awards in 2018. Families are welcome earlier in the evening, while 7:30pm onwards is reserved for adults and older children.

Using local seafood is top-priority for Kelly and Scott, and when they have access to such incredible fresh fish, you can see why. They source crabs and mussels from Frary's, lobsters from Billy Ward and oysters from Richard Loose, and of course they do also serve some 'landlubber' too, which they source from award-winning butcher Arthur Howell.

The bright and light feel from the pale blue décor is complemented by hanging rope lights, and there are a few intriguing ocean-related knick knacks dotted about that create the ideal ambience for tucking into freshly caught seafood.

Part of the excitement with freshly caught seafood is never quite knowing what will be available each day, and this allows the chefs to be inventive with their menus. The specials board changes daily depending on what is in season, and flavouring inspiration comes from all around the globe.

From Norfolk Mussels Mariniere with Bloomer Bread to Tempura King Prawns with Hot Homemade Sweet Chilli Dip and Pickled Ginger Shreds, the starters are all designed to get the tastebuds tingling. For 'the main catch' it can be a struggle to choose between Frary's Dressed Wells Crab or Billy Ward's Steamed Half Lobster... so you can opt for a combination of both, if you like. Other dishes include delights such as skate, hake or turbot, which are cooked to perfection by the skilled chefs.

Wells Crab House
Sri Lankan Crab Curry

A spicy sweet crab curry I learned while participating in a chef's table experience at the amazing Cinnamon Lodge hotel in Habarana, Sri Lanka.

PREPARATION TIME: 15 MINUTES | COOKING TIME: 1 HOUR 15 MINUTES | SERVES 12 (BUT CAN BE FROZEN)

METHOD

Heat the coconut oil in a big pan and add the mustard seeds, dill seeds and curry leaves. Fry until the seeds start to pop, then add the grated ginger, crushed garlic, chopped chillies and onions. Sweat until soft, then stir in all the dry spices and salt. Fry for 5 minutes.

Add the chopped tomatoes, coconut milk, crab meat (use more to taste if needed) and then simmer the curry for 1 hour on a very low heat.

Season with more salt if needed or more coconut milk if the curry is not sweet enough. More crab can be added at any time if the flavour is not present when you taste the sauce.

Serve with zesty lime-scented basmati rice and a red onion and lime salad. This will make quite a lot of curry for domestic use but you can safely freeze it in portions which will keep for 6-8 months. Once defrosted don't panic at the look of it, as the coconut oil will split, but will be fine once reheated.

To do this with chicken, add diced chicken breast at the dry spices stage. To do this with prawns, add cooked and peeled prawns 10 minutes before the end of the cooking time.

INGREDIENTS

4 tbsp coconut oil
2 tbsp yellow mustard seeds
3 tbsp dill seeds
2 tbsp curry leaves
4 large thumbs of ginger, peeled and grated
12 cloves of garlic, crushed
12 red chillies, finely chopped
8 red onions, finely diced
2 tbsp unroasted curry powder
2 tbsp ground turmeric
2 tbsp hot chilli powder
½ tbsp crushed black pepper
4 tsp salt
4 tins of chopped tomatoes
4 tins of coconut milk
12 dressed crabs

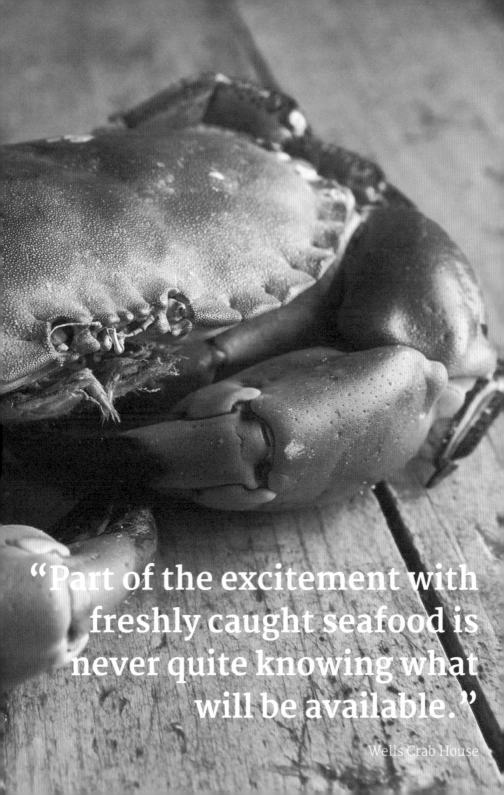

"Part of the excitement with freshly caught seafood is never quite knowing what will be available."

Wells Crab House

Local Food Heroes

For a quaint Cotswolds market town, Nailsworth certainly has a far-reaching reputation when it comes to being something of a gastronomic hot spot. Much of this comes down to the highly celebrated seafood restaurant, fishmonger and delicatessen, William's.

WILLIAM'S FOOD HALL & OYSTER BAR
3 Fountain Street
Nailsworth
GL6 0BL

Telephone: 01453 832240

Website: www. williamsfoodhall. co.uk

Award-winning delicatessen and oyster bar that is one of Rick Stein's Food Heroes and Matthew Fort's 'Five Favourite Places to Shop'.

Completely refurbished in January 2020, the cosy, seafood-themed restaurant at William's now offers over sixty covers complete with handmade leather-upholstered chairs and banquettes, fishermen's lamps, a new cocktail bar and stylish coastal wall art. The restaurant is now open for lunch on Monday to Saturday and dinner every Friday and Saturday evenings. A riverside outdoor terrace is also open in the summer months with Nailsworth's famous willow tree providing dappled shade for diners.

Fresh fish and seafood arrive daily from Cornish day boats onto the famous fish counter. The adjacent delicatessen boasts an outstanding range of cheeses, charcuterie, terrines and chef-prepared meals, alongside a vibrant selection of locally sourced fruits and vegetables, all beautifully displayed.

The William's story began over forty years ago, when William and Rae Beeston opened William's Kitchen at 3 Fountain Street, Nailsworth. Frank Carpenter had a shop there since 1951, selling an array of freshly caught fish from a marble slab in the window, as well as a selection of game such as rabbit, fowl and pheasants, usually seen hanging upside down.

William and Rae's business harnessed the success of Frank's shop and swiftly went from strength to strength as a fishmonger, delicatessen and also a caterer. Soon William's Kitchen was attracting attention from all over the region and even from much further afield. William was named as one of Rick Stein's Food Heroes and the shop also gained recognition as one of Matthew Fort's 'Five Favourite Places to Shop'.

In 2014 it was time for William to step down and retire after an impressive 39 years running his eponymous business. It was bought by local family Ed and Helen Playne, who are passionate about continuing the William's story long into the future and maintaining their reputation for culinary excellence in Nailsworth, the Cotswolds and throughout the whole region.

William's Food Hall
Chargrilled Halibut with Crushed Potatoes & Mediterranean Salsa

Freshly caught fish pairs beautifully with the flavourful combination of crab and new potatoes. Add a zingy salsa and smooth red pepper sauce for a medley of tastes and textures.

PREPARATION TIME: 30 MINUTES | COOKING TIME: 30 MINUTES | SERVES 4

INGREDIENTS

For the salsa
1 bunch of spring onions, diced
1 red pepper, diced
1 yellow pepper, diced
Handful of coriander
50g capers, chopped
50g black olives, chopped
Olive oil
Lemon juice
Salt and pepper

For the pepper sauce
1 shallot
2 red peppers
1 tsp olive oil
1 tsp smoked paprika
1 sprig of thyme
200ml white wine

For the potatoes
50g butter
1 shallot, peeled and diced
150g crab meat (white and brown)
500g new potatoes, cooked and crushed
50ml lemon juice
Chopped parsley

For the halibut
4 x 200g halibut steaks
Olive oil, for cooking
Cooked samphire, to serve

METHOD

For the salsa
Mix all the ingredients together in a bowl, season with salt and pepper and set aside.

For the pepper sauce
Finely chop the shallots and cut the red peppers into small pieces, removing all seeds. Place the shallots in a frying pan with the olive oil and sweat until softened. Add the peppers and continue to fry for another few minutes. Add the thyme and white wine to the pan and simmer for 5 minutes. Blend the mixture in a food processor until smooth.

For the potatoes
Melt the butter in a saucepan, add the shallot and cook gently until golden brown. Add the crab meat and the crushed potatoes and roughly mix together. Once ready to serve, drizzle with lemon juice and add chopped parsley to taste.

For the halibut
Pat the halibut steaks dry and heat a griddle pan until it is very hot. Add some olive oil to the pan and then cook the halibut for around 2-3 minutes on each side. The griddle pan should leave black stripes across the flesh. Check it is cooked through to the middle before serving.

To serve
Place the crab crushed potatoes in the centre of a warmed plate. Place the halibut on top and spoon over the salsa. Heat the red pepper sauce and drizzle it around the fish. Serve with cooked samphire.

Other titles from Meze Publishing

The Manchester Cook Book: Second Helpings features Ben Mounsey of Grafene, Hatch, Refuge, Masons, Old School BBQ Bus and lots more.
978-1-910863-44-2

The Lakes and Cumbria Cook Book Featuring: Shed 1 Distillery, Carvetii, Slate Bar and Café
ISBN: 9781910863305

The Cambridgeshire Cook Book: Second Helpings features Mark Abbott of Midsummer House, The Olive Grove, Elder Street Café and lots more.
978-1-910863-33-6

For the Love of the Sea Featuring: The Female Fisherman, Jane Devonshire, A Passion for Seafood
ISBN: 9781910863756

The Nottingham Cook Book: Second Helpings features Welbeck Estate, Memsaab, Sauce Shop, 200 Degrees Coffee, Homeboys, Rustic Crust and lots more.
978-1-910863-27-5

The Devon Cook Book sponsored by Food Drink Devon features Simon Hulstone of The Elephant, Noel Corston, Riverford Field Kitchen and much more.
978-1-910863-24-4

The South London Cook Book features Jose Pizarro, Adam Byatt, The Alma, Piccalilli Caff, Canopy Beer, Inkspot Brewery and lots more.
978-1-910863-27-5

The Brighton & Sussex Cook Book features Steven Edwards, The Bluebird Tea Co, Isaac At, Real Patisserie, Sussex Produce Co, and lots more.
978-1-910863-22-0

For the Love of the Land 1 Featuring: The Bear and Blacksmith, Tyn Llwyfan Farm, Tractors and Tweed
ISBN: 9781910863589

For the Love of the Land 2 Featuring: Yeo Valley, Glass Brothers, Jekka's Herb Farm
ISBN: 9781910863923

The Leeds Cook Book features The Boxtree, Crafthouse, Stockdales of Yorkshire and lots more.
978-1-910863-18-3

The Cotswolds Cook Book features David Everitt-Matthias of Champignon Sauvage, Prithvi, Chef's Dozen and lots more.
978-0-9928981-9-9

The Shropshire Cook Book features Chris Burt of The Peach Tree, Old Downton Lodge, Shrewsbury Market, CSons and lots more.
978-1-910863-32-9

The Edinburgh & East Coast Cook Book features Jamie Scott from The Newport & Scott Smith from Fhior, Akva, Edinburgh Larder, Kilted Lobster and lots more.
978-1-910863-45-9

Little Book of Cakes and Bakes Featuring: Blanchflower, Ahh Toots, Crust and Crumb
ISBN: 9781910863480

All books in this series are available from Waterstones, Amazon and good independent bookshops.

Find out more about us at www.mezepublishing.co.uk